CHARL[

ESSENTIAL WRITINGS IN S[... THEOLOGY

MW01026447

WORKS BY CHARLES WILLIAMS
FROM WHICH THIS VOLUME WAS COLLECTED:

Descent of the Dove
The Image of the City
He Came Down from Heaven
The Forgiveness of Sins

CHARLES WILLIAMS

Essential Writings in Spirituality and Theology

CHARLES HEFLING, EDITOR

COWLEY PUBLICATIONS

Cambridge ◆ Boston
Massachusetts

Introduction © 1993 by Charles Hefling
All rights reserved.

Published in the United States of America by Cowley Publications, a division of the
Society of St. John the Evangelist. No portion of this book may be reproduced,
stored in or introduced into a retrieval system, or transmitted, in any form or by
any means—including photocopying—without the prior written permission of Cowley
Publications, except in the case of brief quotations embodied in critical articles and
reviews.

International Standard Book Number: 1-56101-073-1
Library of Congress Number: 93-6674

Library of Congress Cataloging-in-Publication Data
Williams, Charles, 1886-1945.
    [Essays. Selections]
    Charles Williams : essential writings in spirituality and theology / Charles He-
fling, editor.
        p. cm.
    Originally published:
    Includes bibliographical references.
    ISBN 1-56101-073-1
    1. Theology. 2. Spirituality. I. Hefling, Charles C. II. Title.
BR85.W568425 1993
230—dc20   93-6674

Material from *The Image of the City and Other Essays, He Came Down From
Heaven, The Descent of the Dove,* and *The Forgiveness of Sins* is reprinted by permission of the estate of the author and the Watkins Loomis Agency.

 This book is printed on recycled, acid-free paper and was produced in the
United States of America.

Cowley Publications
28 Temple Place
Boston, Massachusetts 02111

ACKNOWLEDGMENTS

For her counsel and encouragement, and for providing the text of the statements written for the Companions of the Co-inherence, I am indebted to Mary McDermott Shideler. Special thanks are due to Anne O'Donnell, whose passion for accuracy and eye for detail would have met Williams's own exacting editorial standards.

TABLE OF CONTENTS

THE PATTERN OF THE GLORY

INTRODUCTION

By Charles Hefling

W hen Charles Williams said that "if one is anxious to write about God, one ought to be anxious to write well," he might have been stating his own aspirations. Writing was both his trade and his vocation, and he was always writing about God. Not that everything he wrote is theology. Most of it, in fact, is not. He wrote fiction, seven novels in all; he wrote non-fiction, chiefly history and literary criticism; he wrote, above all, poetry—"whether that is or is not fiction," as he put it. He wrote nearly forty books, all told, three or four of which a librarian would catalogue under "theology." But the conventional classifications are too clumsy to describe what Williams wrote. "All his books," as Dorothy Sayers rightly observed, "illuminate one another, for the same master-themes govern them all, so that it is impossible to confine any one theme to a single book." Nor can any of the books be assigned to a single category.

T.S. Eliot, who like Sayers knew him personally, thought Williams used such a variety of literary forms because "what he had to say was beyond his resources, and probably beyond the resources of language, to say once for all through any one medium of expression." That is not to suggest that what he had to say is elaborate or obscure. It is blazingly simple. As a character remarks in one of the novels, once you have said "Good God!" there is not much else to say. But the ways of saying "Good God!" are endless, and if exploring them is "doing theology" then there is very little in Williams's writing that is *not* theological.

During his life the writing for which he was best known was his literary criticism. Poetry was his special field as a critic, English poetry in particular but also Dante, as we shall see. His own verse, however, is what he would have wished to be remembered for, and "CHARLES WILLIAMS: POET" is inscribed on his tombstone. C.S. Lewis ranked Williams's mature poetry among the two or three most valuable books of verse produced in the twentieth century, although he added, presciently perhaps, that its extreme difficulty might kill it. The novels, on the other hand, are alive and well. They have never been out of print for long, and it is through *All Hallows' Eve* or *The Greater Trumps, Descent Into Hell* or *War In Heaven*, to name my own favorites, that readers today are most likely to have encountered Williams saying "Good God!"

As a novelist Williams is often named in one breath with Lewis and J.R.R. Tolkien, and not without reason. He belonged for a time to the Inklings, the now famous circle of writers of which Tolkien and Lewis were the most famous members. He shared their conviction that a story is sometimes the best way of saying what there is to say, he wrote "fantastic" fiction, as they did, and his tales, like theirs, reflect a Christian outlook. But the comparison only goes so far. Lewis never seems to leave the lecturer's podium; writing fiction is a species of teaching. Tolkien is just the opposite in that narrative, for him, needs no further purpose. Telling a story is an end in itself, and the reason he gives for writing *The Lord of the Rings* is that he wanted to try his hand at telling a really long one. Williams does not fit either mold. Certainly his stories, like Lewis's, are *about* something, other than themselves; but they are not about Christianity in the sense that they translate Christian tenets into imaginative prose. A better way to put it would be that Williams's fiction is about the same things Christianity is about—where we come from, where we are going, and how we get there. In other words, it is about God. But the purpose of the novels is not so much to instruct as to indicate—to call attention to what things are like in fact, by redescribing them in fiction.

In effect, then, though not in form, Williams's novels are poetry, which helps to explain why they are at once more ordinary and more extraordinary—or better, they are more natural and at the same time more supernatural—than *The Lord of the Rings* or Lewis's outer-space trilogy. The plot of a Williams novel turns on events that are as uncanny as anything in Lewis or Tolkien. But where do they happen? Not in the exotic world of a distant age or a distant planet, but in the matter-of-fact, middle-class world of a publishing house, a London suburb, or a sleepy village. And they do not happen to characters who are more or other than human, but to rather unremarkable people—a secretary, a minor civil servant, a butterfly-collector. When the uncanniness begins, it is all the more sublime—or all the more horrible—because of the contrast with the ordinariness that surrounds it. A pterodactyl is much the sort of thing you might expect to see in Tolkien's Middle Earth. It is not what a graduate student writing a dry research thesis on a medieval philosopher expects to see outside her window, as a character does in *The Place of the Lion*.

Someone has called Williams's novels "supernatural thrillers," which fits them well enough, but they are no less serious on that account. As Lewis himself pointed out, "the frank supernaturalism and the frankly blood-curdling episodes" are not there for their shock-value. Although Williams was not an allegorist like Bunyan or a preacher like Milton, his stories do put fiction to use for truthful purposes. Quite often the best commentary on some theological point he makes will be found not elsewhere in his theology but in the novels. Because they make their appeal to imagination, to "the feeling intellect" rather than emotion alone, they can convince the reader as perhaps nothing else could that what they depict is objectively real—that the routine stream of sights and sounds which meets us every day runs deeper than we suppose, and that an intangible dimension exists in, with, and under every moment of our experience. Call this further reality spiritual, if you like, or metaphysical or transcendental. By whatever name it can, if Williams is to be believed, make its presence known and felt at any moment—and it does.

People who knew him personally observed the same coexistence of the mundane and the otherworldly in Williams himself. "I have never met any human being," one of them wrote, "in whom the divisions between body and spirit, natural and supernatural, temporal and eternal were so non-existent, nor any writer who so consistently took their non-existence for granted." Eliot puts a similar impression on record in his introduction to *All Hallows' Eve*, arguably the best of Williams's novels. "To him the supernatural was perfectly natural, and the natural was also supernatural. And this peculiarity gave him that profound insight into Good and Evil, into the heights of Heaven and the depths of Hell, which provides both the immediate thrill, and the permanent message of his novels."

The writings collected here display the same insight and perhaps also, in their own less dramatic way, the same thrill. None of them is fiction, although some discuss fiction. All of them are about facts, and all of them are about God, which for Williams amounts to the same thing. Every fact is a theological fact, simply because it *is* a fact. "The glory of God," Williams declares, "is in facts. The almost incredible nature of things is that there is no fact which is not in his glory." In those two sentences he lays the foundation on which everything in this volume is built. The rest of my introduction will be an attempt to explain what they mean.

"Glory" is the place to begin. It is one of Williams's favorite words, and he uses it in a sense of his own. The "mazy bright blur" that people commonly associate with glory is not exactly what he has in mind. Amazement, yes; brightness, yes; but not blurry indistinctness. "The maze should be...exact, and the brightness should be that of a geometrical pattern." Glory is like what you see through a kaleidoscope rather than what you see through a fog. It is precise and regular, like a solemn liturgy or an intricate dance, which are two of the images Williams uses in his novels for the all-inclusive orderliness that bespeaks the divine. Another, which appears in his non-fictional writing as well, is the image of a city. Places and buildings, each distinct yet connected with the others by a network of paths, and a multitude of persons with different roles to play and a jobs to do, all coordinated with the others in a vastly complex web of interdependence—that, for Williams, is an earthly counterpart of heaven.

As though to emphasize that glory is not just splendor but orderly splendor, Williams often speaks of "the pattern of the glory." It is one of his most characteristic phrases, and I have made it the title of this introduction. The web of relationships that he means by *pattern* is intelligible, but the intelligence needed to grasp it is not the kind computers imitate. Perceiving in facts the glory of God is as much a matter of aesthetic intuition as of logical reasoning. Perhaps the best analogy would be understanding poetry: facts are the words, God is the poet, and the world, past and present, is the poem. If this universal poem is to be rightly construed, all the words—every fact—must be accounted for. Each has a place in the whole and none may be overlooked. And if it is to be construed in terms of its author's intention, as a poem should be, the terms must be God's rather than ours, "the terms he deigns to apply, not the terms we force on him. And this, it seems, is the use of all science—to discover his own terms." Far from thinking of the "secular" sciences as opposed to theology, Williams held their pursuit of accurate, factual knowledge in high esteem as an exploration of divine glory.

That "the glory of God is in facts" is the theme on which the essays in this volume are variations. Some of the facts Williams writes about are historical facts; some, the second World War for example, were occurring even as he wrote. Some are permanent, and some are always occurring. Spiritual facts are included, of course. Nobody had a stronger sense than he of the reality of forgiveness, charity, and redemption, sin and damnation, "the heights of Heaven and the depths of Hell." At the same time, nobody was more vividly aware, either, of the divine glory of material facts, not least the facts of sensuality and sex. The body, he insists, "was holily created, is holily redeemed, and is to be holily raised from the dead. It is, in fact, for all our difficulties with it, less fallen, merely in itself, than the soul."

That is why he found D.H. Lawrence, that "convinced and rhetorical heretic" as he called him, worth paying attention to. Lawrence exaggerated, as heretics always do; it is what makes them heretical. But he erred on the right side. The body in general, and sexuality in particular, have generally been given low grades by religious and philosophical teachers. Plato is a prime example, but even Christians, who ought to know better, have too often regarded the flesh as at best a nuisance and a distraction. For the most part they have said the right things, officially at least, but in the wrong tone, so that the youngster Williams quotes can be excused for asking, "Isn't marriage rather a wicked sacrament?" Williams did not think so. Merely in itself, the body is less fallen than the soul, and merely in itself he calls it, following Wordsworth, an "index." The words in a printed index are meaningful in themselves while at the same time they also point beyond themselves to the meaning of the whole book. Likewise, the material existence of "the holy and glorious flesh" has a significance of its own, which also indicates the corresponding significance of the whole material world. That is what Lawrence was able to see, even though he had not much understanding of the reasons why it is there to be seen.

The first essay in this volume is about those reasons. "Natural Goodness" is Williams in a nutshell, or as close to it as anything he wrote. It draws an outline to which the rest of this collection adds depth and detail, and I have put it at the beginning on that account. It has the defects of its virtues, however. Because it is so compact, readers who are unfamiliar with the way Williams thinks and writes may find it a little daunting. If so, I recommend beginning with one of the more specific items instead—with "Sensuality and Substance," for example, where the discussion of Lawrence appears; or with the book review "Augustine and Athanasius," which like many of the reviews Williams wrote tells as much about his own ideas as about the books reviewed; or with "The Cross," probably the most personal essay in this collection. But almost any of the others will serve. What Sayers said of Williams's books is equally true of these shorter writings: the same master-themes govern them all.

One of those themes is the main point in "Natural Goodness": natural, material things are expressive in their own right. In making this point, however, Williams also gives its theological explanation. Matter is a *creature*, a created reality. But to be created involves having, and so referring to, a creator; and Williams argues that the physical creature called matter refers no less surely than does the immaterial creature called spirit. The sheer fact of existing, physically or spiritually, is meaningful. There is more than an echo here of the protest raised by nineteenth-century romanticism against the idea that matter is good for nothing except to be manipulated for economic ends by technological means. But it would be equally true to say that Williams was ahead of his time. He would have found much to approve of in the creation spirituality that is flourishing at the end of the twentieth century.

His high doctrine of creation, in any case, does not stand alone, for although natural goodness is a fact, natural facts are not the only facts. On one side, the side of the creatures, there is the fact of "the chosen catastrophe which we call the Fall"; on the other, the fact that "the Creator had to become a Savior lest his creation should be wholly lost." Three points thus define the pattern within which the holiness of matter has its explanation, corresponding to the three acts of the biblical drama—creation, fall, redemption. Nothing all that remarkable so far. But Williams's reading of the drama in "Natural Goodness" is not the conventional one, although it is certainly a Christian reading. Theologians are agreed that the way in which the Creator became a Savior was to unite himself with the created, with matter in flesh. Usually, though, they go on to explain that it was *because* of the Fall that God became incarnate, whereas Williams takes the position that the Incarnation would have occurred, Fall or no Fall. Being united with matter was the Creator's intention all along. It is why he created at all. To say that matter is good because it was so created is true, then, as far as it goes, but there is a reason why it has been so created. That reason is the Incarnation.

About the Incarnation, in itself, Williams has little to say. The union of the Creator with the created is in the strict sense of the word a mystery, and he was deeply suspicious of mere speculation in such matters. There is, however, one thing he does say about the Incarnation, and he says it often, usually by quoting the Athanasian Creed. This "great humanist ode," as he called it, is not so familiar as the other Christian creeds, but the Book of Common Prayer in use when Williams wrote calls for it to be recited on certain festivals. Here is the description in *The Greater Trumps* of a country church choir singing it on Christmas Day:

> The mingled voices of men and boys were proclaiming the nature of Christ—"God and man is one Christ'; then the boys fell silent, and the men went on, "One, not by conversion of the Godhead into flesh, but by taking of the manhood into God." On the assertion they ceased, and the boys rushed joyously in, "One altogether, not"—they looked at the idea and tossed it airily away—"*not* by confusion of substance, but by unity"—they rose, they danced, they triumphed—"by unity, by unity"—they were silent, all but one, and that one fresh perfection proclaimed the full consummation, each syllable rounded, prolonged, exact— "by unity of person."

Williams obviously loved the creed for its crisp precision, among other things. In Christ, Creator and created, deity and humanity, have become one in a definite way, which can be unambiguously stated: "not by conversion of the Godhead into flesh, but by taking of the manhood into God." This clause in particular shows up again and again in Williams's prose, and the distinction it draws is no quibble. Should we think of the Incarnation as a contraction of deity, a "conversion of the Godhead into flesh"? Or was it, as the creed specifies, an intensification of humanity, a "taking of the manhood into God"? It makes all the difference, and something of what the difference amounts to can be gathered from the second piece in this collection, "The Incarnation of the Kingdom."

Broadly speaking, this chapter is a re-presentation, with commentary, of the gospel narrative, drawn mainly from Mark and John. But nothing could be more thoroughly at odds with a run-of-the-mill life-of-Jesus approach. Williams scarcely mentions the name "Jesus." He seldom does. As a rule he prefers a title, often "Messias." Why not "Christ"? Many readers, I suspect, have asked that; at least one irritated reviewer did. If nothing but a title would do, what was wrong with the one everybody knows? To which I think the most likely answer is that everybody does know it, and that is what was wrong. Williams, poet that he was, wanted a word unusual enough to be arresting; a word, in fact, that might have something of the same effect "Christ" has when it makes its earliest appearance, abruptly and without explanation, in the earliest gospel. "No doubt when we have looked up annotated editions and biblical dictionaries, we know what 'the Christ' means....But at the moment, there, it is a kind of incantation, the invocation of a ritual, antique, and magical title." This strangeness has long since worn off, and thanks to Handel even "Messiah" is familiar. But the peculiar form "Messias" still calls attention to itself, and its very oddness helps Williams make one of his main points in "The Incarnation of the Kingdom." Briefly stated, it is that the gospels present a Christ as enigmatic as his title.

The enigma is for Williams an essential part of the meaning of the Incarnation. In Christ God has, certainly, been made like us. Williams had no doubt about that, or about the gratitude and love which that likeness has evoked. Still, he adds, "there is at least equal satisfaction that it is an unlike us who is so made. It is an alien Power which is caught and suspended in our very midst." To condemn the aloof, impersonal Christ of Byzantine icons is all very well, but to replace them with the uninterestingly ordinary Jesus of so many modern accounts is at least as much a distortion, and in Williams's judgment a more pernicious one. With "immature and romantic devotions to the simple Jesus, the spiritual genius, the broad-minded international Jewish working-man, the falling-sparrow and grass-of-the-field Jesus," he had small sympathy. "They will not serve. The Christian idea from the beginning had believed that his Nature reconciled earth and heaven, and all things met in him, God and Man. A Confucian Wordsworth does not help here."

In stressing the otherness of Jesus so relentlessly—to the point of calling him "the Divine Thing" and using neuter pronouns, as though personality itself would make him, or it, too familiar—Williams is objecting to a domesticated Christ, a Christ made bland in hopes of making Christianity easier to swallow. Cutting the "alien Power" of God incarnate down to manageable size is one thing that falls under the rubric of "converting the Godhead into flesh." Yet for all his stress on the deity of Christ, Williams by no means minimizes the humanity. He does relocate it, though. Unlike the doctrine of Christ as God, which was worked out, with its corollaries, and definitively settled long ago, "the other doctrine of his manhood, with its corollaries, has still to be worked out and put into action," and Williams is himself working it out in much of his writing. Its corollaries, however, do not regard the human Jesus so much as the humanity that in Jesus has been taken into God.

It is in working out some of these corollaries that Williams makes one of his most original and lasting contributions to

Christian thought: his theology of romantic love. The fact that the divine Being who is Love itself has become one with the humanity he created means, among other things, that "any human energy...is capable of being assumed into sacramental and transcendental heights—such is the teaching of the Incarnation." It may be only once in a life that the body with its physical energies reveals a transcendent meaning so as to become, for that moment, a kind of divine incarnation. But, rare though they are, such moments do occur, and their occurrence is perhaps least rare in a lover's experience of the beloved. On that experience Williams built his romantic theology.

Sayers tells the story of Williams having his hair cut and hearing the barber say that when his sweetheart was with him he felt he had not an enemy in the world and could forgive anyone for anything. Whereupon Williams jumped from the chair to shout, "My dear man, that's exactly what Dante said!" Her anecdote makes two points that are worth noting. The first is that Williams's theology of romantic love is anchored solidly in the human condition rather than the shifting sand of a particular culture or period. "The thing happens," he was fond of saying, and it happens without regard to this or that place and time. Six hundred years separate his barber from Dante, and fourteenth-century Florence was quite a different milieu from twentieth-century London, yet the barber could, in his own way, say exactly what Dante said in magnificent verse, because both had found themselves in the same state of affairs. Each had fallen in love.

The second point regards Dante himself. That "the thing happens" is important, but far more important is what happens *next*. The moment of romantic love can be an end or a beginning. To take it as an end, as complete in itself, is "the preference of an immediately satisfying experience of things to the believed pattern of the universe; one may even say, the pattern of the glory." It is a preference that Williams identifies with sin. But such a moment can instead be a beginning, a question in search of an answer; and that is where Dante comes in. For Williams the one and only question to ask about the state of being in love is the question Dante asked: "is it serious? is it capable of intellectual treatment?...Is it (in some sense or other) *true*?" And his answer had a deep and lasting effect on Williams's own intellectual treatment of romantic love, which appears most comprehensively in *The Figure of Beatrice*, regarded by many as the finest of his books. There are also shorter versions, though, and a Williams anthology without at least one of them would be like the proverbial princeless *Hamlet*.

The one included here is from *He Came Down from Heaven*, which Williams dedicated to his wife, "with whom I began to study the doctrine of glory." In "The Theology of Romantic Love" he relates the pattern of that glory, as he discovered it both in Dante and in his own experience, to the pattern of the Incarnation of Love. They are, or ought to be, the same pattern, for reasons which are at the very heart of Williams's understanding of Christianity. He states them succinctly in "Saint John" when he says the fourth gospel "particularly stresses the fact that all the events in the life of our Lord, as well as happening in Judea, happen in the soul." There is an indissoluble connection between *what happened* in history and *what is happening* in the individual. Not only do they mirror each other, so that "the historical events...are a pageant of the events of the human soul," but also they do happen because they did happen. Had they never existed outwardly in the past they could not exist inwardly in the present.

But the inward events that constitute romantic love have another, more immediate outward cause as well. What happens in the lover's soul happens because of the beloved. And because it happens, not in a single moment but as the unfolding of a story, romantic love has a narrative shape that may, and should, conform with the shape of the gospel narrative. "The beloved...becomes the Mother of Love; Love is born in the soul; it may have its passion there; it may have its resurrection there. It has its own divine nature united with our undivine nature." In the lover as in Judea the kingdom becomes incarnate. Two natures become one, as they did in Christ; and like its original in history this incarnation in the individual takes place, not by the conversion of the Godhead into flesh, but by the taking of humanity into God.

In assigning so crucial a place in his theology to the moment of romantic love Williams is not claiming it is the one and only point of entry into the pattern of the glory. "Romantic love between the sexes," he readily admits, "is but one kind of romantic love, which is but a particular habit of Romanticism as a whole, which is itself but a particular method of the Affirmation of Images." The almost incredible nature of things is that there is no fact that is not in the glory of God, and therefore no fact that cannot be affirmed as an image. For Dante the fact around which everything revolved was a person, Beatrice, who "was, in her degree, an image of nobility, of virtue, of the Redeemed Life, in some sense of Almighty God himself." Williams does not mean that she was *like* nobility, virtue, the redeemed life, the Almighty. She was like nothing but herself. For just that reason, however—because she was entirely and exclusively the person she was and no other—she could be an *image*. The same is true of every image, in Williams's sense of the word. Like a sacrament or an index, an image includes and makes present the thing of which it is an image, so that for Dante to behold Beatrice was to behold beatitude and nothing less. Yet the image does not cease to be uniquely and wholly itself. Together with an identity there is always an otherness.

As a way of apprehending transcendence, the Way of the Affirmation of Images is associated with one of the aphorisms that are such a characteristic feature of Williams's writing. To affirm an image as a revelation of God is to say, "this also is Thou." But because an image conceals even as it discloses, any such affirmation must always be corrected by adding its opposite: "neither is this Thou." As the first phrase is the maxim of the Affirmative Way in general and of romantic love in particular, so too the second conveys the essence of another, complementary spirituality, which Williams calls the Way of the Negation (or Rejection) of Images. To the Negative Way belong asceticism and self-denial, wordless, imageless prayer, and the mystical ascent to a "cloud of unknowing." Neither of these Ways is entirely independent of the other, and their watchwords are the two halves of one saying, which Williams treats as a quotation although he never found its source: *this also is Thou; neither is this Thou*. "As a maxim for living," he said of this formula, "it is invaluable, and it—or its reversal—summarizes the history of the Christian Church."

As such it serves as a motto for *The Descent of the Dove*, Williams's own history of the church. This remarkable book has been called the only imaginative church history ever written, but its subtitle gives a description that is perhaps more illuminating. By calling it *A Short History of the Holy Spirit in the Church*, Williams was committing what he no doubt knew was a theological solecism, for since the Holy Spirit is God and God is by definition timeless, a history of the Spirit is a contradiction in terms. Nevertheless I think that he meant what he said, and that the paradox he put into his subtitle gives a clue to his whole approach as a historian of Christianity. On the one hand, the hope he voices at the beginning of *Descent* is what any good historian would hope, namely that "all the dates and details are accurate" and that "the curve of history has been justly followed." On that score there is no cause for complaint. But even so, on the other hand, the curve of history as Williams follows it takes the form of a life being lived out by one being with one personality. *Descent of the Dove* invites comparison with the biographies Williams wrote, for in much the same way that a biography presents its subject's essential character by presenting a historical narrative of the deeds in which that character is embodied, so a history of the church, as Williams conceives it, will disclose the essential character of its divine Subject, "our Lord the Spirit," in and through a sequence of events in the world of human affairs.

He did not find it coincidental, for example, that no sooner had the Way of Affirmation reached its highest literary peak than the Way of Negation was similarly brought to consummate expression. For the first of these achievements Dante was responsible; for the second, the unknown—in Williams's opinion, the very appropriately unknown—author of *The Cloud of Unknowing.* That two writers so utterly different should have written within a few years of each other is not really surprising, if you grant that the operation of Christendom is, as Williams held it to be, a *co*operation of human persons with the divine Person of the Spirit in one corporate whole. Indeed you would expect, on that hypothesis, to find Christian spirituality advancing along the Ways of Affirmation and Negation at the same pace so as to reach its double consummation at the same time.

Another such unsurprising coincidence appears in "The Renewal of Contrition," a chapter from *The Descent of the Dove* included here. One year, 1534, saw the German Bible published, the Jesuits founded, and the *Institutes of the Christian Religion* drafted. The individuals concerned, Luther, Ignatius of Loyola, and Calvin, had gone through a conversion—one conversion, Williams suggests, rather than three.

"It pleased our Lord the Spirit violently to convulse these souls with himself. Grace seized on those strategic centers for its own campaign." The object of the campaign was the renewal of contrition that gives this chapter its title. Williams calls it "the real reformation, of which the Reformation generally so called is but a small part," and finds its "strategic centers" more alike than other church historians of his day were wont to acknowledge. The difference is partly a matter of perspective and emphasis, but partly also of metaphysics. The sixteenth-century renewal as he portrays it happened not just *in* Christendom but *to* Christendom, as a whole, and it happened everywhere at once. Williams does not ignore internal divisions and confessional conflicts, but whether institutional or intellectual they were not enough to undermine his conviction that there has never ceased to be such a thing—one thing—as Christendom.

It is a conviction that rests on two grounds. First, there is the oneness of the Spirit whose biography is the history of the church. But if Christendom depends for its unity on the cooperation of its citizens with the Holy Ghost, it depends as well, and equally, on the cooperation of its citizens with one another. Williams was in his own way as much a political as a romantic theologian. The image of the city is as prominent in his writing as the image of the beloved, and for the same reason. As in love affairs, so also in civil affairs the natural order of things merges with the supernatural to become eternity's presence in time. But the natural order includes social structures, institutions, customs, and every other organizing of human activity. In a word, it includes civilization. Like sexuality, civilization can be raised to transcendent heights, and as so raised it is what Williams means by Christendom.

The key to all this is "co-inherence." The word is a kind of Williams trademark, and the idea animates nearly all that he wrote. He borrowed both from the theology of the Trinity, where co-inherence refers to the way each of the divine persons lives in and through the other two, inseparably one with them while remaining distinct. That is what it is to *be* a divine person—to exist mutually, to have a personal identity that consists entirely in being related to other persons—and so it also defines what a human person is meant to be. Co-inherence, in other words, is the principle both of the incomprehensible mystery of the three personal Individualities who nevertheless exist as one God, and of the plain, if neglected, truth that human being is being-from and being-in other persons.

In the Trinity, co-inherence is an eternal fact; in humankind, a natural fact. When those two facts meet the result is a third, supernatural fact, the co-inherence of the kingdom, of Christendom, of the church. Williams describes it most succinctly in the postscript of *The Descent of the Dove*, which brings the history of the church into the present by suggesting that a new religious order might be founded to stress the pattern and affirm the image of co-inherent life exhibited in that history. The name Williams proposed for this group has been given to the postscript as it appears in this collection: "The Order of the Co-inherence." As to the order's formal structure, he felt that the less of it there was, the better. But not long after publishing *Descent of the Dove*, which is dedicated to the Companions of the Co-inherence, he did go so far as to draw up a list of seven statements, printed here at the end of "The Order of the Co-inherence," that would amount to a constitution if it did not begin by declaring that "the Order has no constitution except in its members." Each of the seven ends with a quotation solemnly introduced by the words "As it was said...." One of these is from Dante, but most are from Scripture and all revolve around vicarious action and vicarious suffering, as an idea but especially as a way of life. Co-inherence, natural and supernatural, is not only a fact but a possibility that has to be made actual by being deliberately enacted.

Together with the list that follows it, "The Order of the Coinherence" marks a transition to the essays in the second half of this volume, which develop the same theme. "The doctrine of the Christian church depends," according to Williams, "on the substitution, in the last experiences, of our sacred Lord for us. The activity of the Christian church may have to recover, more than is commonly supposed, our substitution, one for the other." The recovery he envisioned would involve taking literally the Pauline precept "bear ye one another's burdens" and, what is more, applying it to burdens that are other than physical. As it is possible to carry someone else's groceries, so Williams thought it possible to carry, say, someone else's fear. One of the characters in *Descent Into Hell* does just that. A poet and playwright named Peter Stanhope learns that an acquaintance, Pauline Anstruther, has on several occasions encountered a *Doppelgänger*, an exact double of herself, and lives in constant terror of meeting it again. Has she never, he inquires, asked a friend to carry her fear for her? And might he volunteer himself? At length Pauline agrees to try, if only to please him, and as she leaves for home he sets about keeping his side of the promise.

> Stanhope, turning his eyes from her parting figure,...settled himself more comfortably in his chair. A certain superficial attention, alert and effective in its degree, lay at the disposal of anyone who might need it, exactly as his body was prepared to draw in its long outstretched legs if anyone wanted to pass. Meanwhile he disposed the rest of his attention according to his promise. He recollected Pauline; he visualized her going along a road, any road; he visualized another Pauline coming to meet her. As he did so his mind contemplated not the first but the second Pauline; he took trouble to apprehend the vision, he summoned

through all his sensations an approaching fear. Deliberately he opened himself to that fear, laying aside for
awhile every thought of why he was doing it, forgetting
every principle and law, absorbing only the strangeness
and the terror of that separate spiritual identity....He sat
on, imagining to himself the long walk with its sinister possibility, the ogreish world lying around, the air with its
treachery to all sane appearance. His own eyes began to
seek and strain and shrink, his own feet, quiet though actually they were, began to weaken with the necessity of advance upon the road down which the girl was passing. The
body of his flesh received her alien terror, his mind carried
the burden of her world. The burden was inevitably lighter
for him than for her, for the rage of a personal resentment
was lacking. He endured her sensitiveness, but not her sin;
the substitution there, if indeed there is a substitution, is
hidden in the central mystery of Christendom which Christendom itself has never understood, nor can.

Meanwhile, Pauline is startled to realize that for the first time
in years she has walked home without once feeling dread at
the thought her *Doppelgänger* might appear.

Williams makes a point of saying in the novel that whether
the apparition that had terrified Pauline was an actual being
or a figment is irrelevant. Either way, her terror was an actual
burden, which Stanhope actually felt in her place. And while
all this occurs in a fictional setting, there is every reason to
think that Williams based his description in the novel on
something he had known to occur in fact. Certainly he recommends variations on this practice of "substitution" so often
and so earnestly that it is hard not to believe he had first-
hand evidence of its possibility. But in any case it is not only
his own experience that he draws on in discussing the way of
exchange. Even the fictional passage I have just quoted links
Stanhope's substitution of himself for Pauline with "the cen-

tral mystery of Christendom," that is, with Christ crucified. One of the statements for the Companions of the Co-inherence puts it plainly: the order "includes in the Divine Substitution of Messias all forms of exchange and substitution, and it invokes this Act as the root of all."

The whole pattern of the glory grows out of this act, in which Christ bore for others a burden that in no way belonged to him. In theology the burden has a name—sin—but there has never been an authoritative pronouncement as to what exactly sin consists in, and the same is true of the atonement for sin that Christ made by dying. Each has been explained in different ways by different theologians, though all agree that in order to make sense of either one it is necessary to make sense of the other. Williams has his own way of making sense of both, and it bears directly or indirectly on several of the essays towards the end of this collection. His is by no means a facile understanding of sin and atonement, and it depends in part on ideas he develops in writings that could not be included here. For both these reasons it may be helpful to outline some of the most important points.

Williams begins traditionally enough. He defines sin by its origin, the "chosen catastrophe" called the Fall, and for his account of that he goes to the book of Genesis. Right away it needs to be said that he does not think it makes much difference whether Genesis is history or myth. For one thing, its account is confirmed in either case by "the facts of present human existence." For another, there is a sense in which "history is itself a myth; to the imaginative, engaged in considering these things, all is equally myth. We may issue from it into other judgements—doctrinal, moral, historic. But so doing we enter into another kind of thought and judge by other tests—more important perhaps, but not the same." The meaning of a story such as Genesis tells has to be grasped imaginatively, irrespective of historical judgment.

The judgments that Williams himself derives are doctrinal, and chief among them is one that "Natural Goodness" mentions: "The definition of the Fall is that man determined to know good as evil." Behind this lies a reading of the first three chapters of Genesis that is a perceptive and as unconventional as his reading of the gospels in "The Incarnation of the Kingdom." He adopts the approach of a literary critic, taking the story as it stands in the Bible without presuming to know in advance what it ought to be saying, and calls attention to three points. First, the "fruit of the tree" would, if eaten, bring an increase of knowledge, a knowledge of good *and* evil. Second, to have such knowledge would be to know differently, to know "as gods." Third, this godlike mode of knowing was forbidden to the man and the woman, whom Williams refers to collectively as "the Adam," to emphasize their co-inherence with each other and with humankind.

The Adam knew, then, that there was a knowledge above and beyond their own, that obtaining it would be disaster, and that refusing it belonged to the good which was their relationship to the Creator. Why was it forbidden at all? Not out of arbitrariness, but because "to know as gods" was an impossibility; indeed its being an impossibility and its being forbidden are identical. For God, whose knowing is by sheer intelligence, it is possible to know good not only in itself but in its deprivation—possible, that is, to know evil—without thereby bringing the deprivation into existence. It was not possible for the Adam, whose knowing was experiential. They wanted it, all the same; wanted to know a schism in the universe, a contradiction of the good they already knew; wanted to know evil. "Since there was not—since there never has been and never will be—anything else than the good to know, they knew the good as antagonism." And since what they had wanted to know they could not possibly know as God does, by intellect alone, they knew it in the only way they could

know it, which was the same as the way they already knew
the good—by experience. "They had what they wanted. That
they did not like it when they got it does not alter the fact
that they certainly got it."

Such, in brief, is Williams's reading of what he calls "the
myth of the alteration of knowledge." It depends on the idea
that evil is a negation of good, and it defines sin as a determination to *know* good negatively. Nothing in this definition ex-
plains sin, in the sense of saying why the choice to know
good as evil occurs. The choosing is a possibility, because the
human will is free, but the thing chosen, knowledge of evil, is
not a possibility, because the human mind knows through experience and until the choice is made there is no evil to be experienced. Sin is the only human choice that generates its
own object. When you have said "Good God!" there is really
nothing else to say, unless it is "No!" It is a lie, and that lie is
the original sin.

The main point to keep in mind when reading Williams on
substitution, reconciliation, or pardon is that he finds the
root of the human predicament in a decision on the part of
the human soul to deny the goodness of good. The soul—not
the body. Physical desire is not at fault. "Our bodies are innocent compared to our souls, and their guiltiness is but that
which they are compelled to borrow from the fallen will."
This squares, of course, with Williams's emphasis on the
goodness of matter in itself. But though matter is not the
source of human evil, it is affected by human evil, and this in
turn affects the union with God for which matter was created
in the first place. The contradiction introduced by the Adam
had to be undone, in other words, if the Creator's original intention of becoming one with the matter he created was to be
carried through.

All this may seem a heavy dose of abstruse theology. So, in
a sense, it is. But what Williams says about another theologi-

cal technicality, the argument on faith and works, applies equally here: "it is a matter like most theology—of everyday life." For the name of the act that undoes the Adam's willful lie and reverses the effects of the Fall is simple enough. It is forgiveness.

The Forgiveness of Sins is the last book of theology Williams published, and the two chapters included here are grouped with some essays, also from the early 1940s, that have related concerns. The date is significant. In a world at war there could be no minimizing, much less ignoring, the fact of humanly inflicted evil. Inevitably, the specific allusions and examples used in these essays will seem dated. Yet what Williams says in connection with events of his own day can be transposed to ours with no loss of meaning, and that for two reasons. Like his theology of romantic love, his theology of forgiveness has a validity that wears well over time, because, like the romantic theology, it is a spirituality as well as a philosophy, and because the question it endeavors to address is not confined to any particular era. It is a question as old as the book of Job, from which Williams drew the moral that asking such questions of God has God's own approval. Why is evil allowed to exist? The answer Williams gives is perhaps the only answer there is, and certainly the only one a Christian may give. Evil exists to be forgiven. Though not, in itself, any part of the Creator's plan, evil is nevertheless a fact. But the glory of God is in facts, and "the union of all citizens of the City is not to leave out any facts. Everything that has ever happened is to be a part of it." Somehow, then, even the fact of evil has to be built into the pattern of the glory. That is what happened on the cross, and it is what happens in forgiveness.

The principle of forgiveness as Williams presents it is that ills are cured by their opposites. Since it is the Fall that has to be reversed, the reversal will occur where the Fall occurred, and forgiveness will be the same kind of thing as what is forgiven, only turned inside-out. Now sin, as Williams conceives it, is a deliberately chosen mode of knowing, a disposition that both causes and is caused by a decision to regard things in a certain way. Reverse the ill, then, and you have the cure: in the same way that sin is knowing the good as evil and experiencing it so, forgiveness is knowing experienced evil as good.

More exactly, to forgive is to regard an evil as an occasion for good and thus as a means to good. This is the sense in which evils exist to be forgiven. It follows that the old saying is mistaken. To forgive is *not* to forget; for Williams it is precisely to remember. Forgiveness is a consciousness of sin, in love. The reversal it brings about is not obliteration. Nor could it be. A sin is an event in history, and history cannot be made to run backwards; once an event has occurred, it can never again be true that it has not occurred. To forget a sin that has occurred may at times be all that a given person can manage, but the real question remains. Will it go on occurring? Will it continue to infect the co-inherent history of humankind? And the answer depends, not on whether the sin is remembered or forgotten, but on *how* it is remembered.

There can be, Williams writes, "only two attitudes towards the sin of another towards oneself; one is to entertain a grudge, the other is not to entertain a grudge." Each is a way of remembering. To entertain a grudge is to prolong the injury, to extend its life by nursing it with the feelings it feeds on. Not to entertain a grudge is to invert the Adam's decision, to know "after the mode of heaven," to re-identify oneself with the good. Offense is reversed, in other words, not in the offender but in the offended. This is a hard saying. It violates an intuitive sense of justice. Surely, we are apt to feel, it is up to the sinner to undo the sin. But for Williams justice is not the issue at stake. In the first place, the gospels "make it impossible for a child of the kingdom, for a Christian, to talk of justice or injustice so far as he personally is concerned." In the second, the very question of justice, of who deserves what, assumes that offender and offended, sinner and victim, exist separately. But suppose they do not. Suppose they exist co-inherently, in and through each other. Which of them "ought" to repent, and which to pardon, would no longer be the main thing; all that would matter is that repentance and forgiveness should happen. Indeed repentance and forgiveness themselves would not be separate acts—and for Williams they are not. They are aspects of one event and one state of mind. He equates them explicitly when he writes of "the consciousness of repentance—that is, the consciousness of sin in love; that is, of the forgiveness of sin." *Whose* consciousness? It does not matter, compared with whether such a conscious awareness comes to be.

Forgiveness is thus one way in which it is possible to carry another's burden, perhaps the most important way and surely the most mysterious. Yet "the thing happens," as Williams said of romantic love, and it happens for the same reason romantic love does. "All the events in the life of our Lord, as well as happening in Judea, happen in the soul," and forgiveness is one of them. In the same way that in Williams's romantic theology the progress of love has the shape of the Incarnation, so too in his theology of forgiveness the progress of pardon has the shape of the cross. The human decision to know "as gods" has been countered by the divine decision that God incarnate would know as man. As the Adam willed to know good as evil, so Christ was willing to know evil as good—to forgive. So it was that in the climax of the gospel "the Thing that was, and had always been, and must always be; the fundamental humanity of all men;...the Thing that was Christ Jesus, knew all things in the deprivation of all goodness." And in that state of abandonment and experienced evil, Williams writes, that Christ forgave: "forgave? say, he loved and renewed those who had brought him into it....He so forgave that he exchanged his love for man's loss; he received the loss and gave the love. It is the mere definition of forgiveness."

Half a century has passed since Charles Williams ceased to write—long enough to make his theology seem distant, not long enough to invest it with the sanctity of a classic. It is natural to ask whether he still speaks to our condition, and what there is to hear if he does. Certainly there are particular ideas and emphases that fit with concerns that are much in the minds of Christians today; the positive light, for example, in which sexuality appears in Way of the Affirmation of Images. Certainly too, there are ideas and emphases that do not seem to fit, but may for that reason merit all the more serious consideration; Williams's out-of-step portrayal of Christ, for example, or the way he ranks charity and forgiveness, as Christian virtues, ahead of justice.

Even more than such specific themes, however, the quality that I think commends Williams's thought to the attention of Christians today is its wholeness. He brings together what to the fractious temperament of our time are irreconcilable opposites—doctrine and experience, creed and spirituality, what has happened in history and what is happening in the individual. His Christianity is thoroughly orthodox; far from being impatient with the ancient dogmas of the church he regards them as "the only explanation and the only hope"—precisely because he never separates the supernatural realities they refer to from the natural realities that everyone encounters every day. "Christianity and life ought to be one; no doubt, essentially, they *are* one." The dogmas do nothing more—and nothing less—than state what living humanly is all about. "The Christian church has been charged with the great secrets which are the only facts of existence," facts that are "as broad as creation, as high as the topmost movement of the soul, as deep as the genesis of the blood." That is why Williams calls the Athanasian Creed, seemingly the epitome of arid and dogmatic hair-splitting, a humanist ode. It is also why, on the one hand, he could maintain as firmly as anyone that there is no salvation outside the church or apart from Christ, and on the other that "where there is love, there is Christ; where there is human reconciliation, there is the church."

Love and reconciliation, romance and forgiveness, are the twin poles around which I have tried to arrange this introduction. Its aim has been to give first-time travelers a map of some though by no means all of the landmarks in the terrain of Williams's theology—co-inherence, the Ways of Affirmation and Rejection, the holiness of material things, romantic theology, substitution, sin and forgiveness, Christendom. It may be a good idea to mention as well some hazards that could impede travel. I began with Williams's comment that writing well ought to be the concern of anyone concerned to write about God. How far he achieved this aspiration is of course a question of taste. *Le style c'est l'homme même*, as he quotes the proverb; the style *is* the writer, nowhere more than in his own case. No writer's style pleases every palate, but there are some writers whose style is an acquired taste. Williams is one of them.

He would not, I think, have wanted it otherwise. Although he groups himself with writers "who only repeat, more or less intelligibly, with more or less goodwill, what they have been told," he declines to follow the fashion of that set, which, he says, "is to talk religion precisely as in other sets they talk films or finance." Such talk, and such writing, has its use. But immediate appeal was never Williams's concern even in writing fiction, much less in writing explicitly about God. I do not mean that he was willfully obscure; far from it. But neither is his the superficial clarity of a newspaper column on movies or money that is meant to be read quickly and at most once.

He was a great phrasemaker, for one thing; only G.K. Chesterton is in the same league. The aphorisms and epigrams that are hallmarks of his prose make reading it anything but dull, but they can also be distractions. Pithy statements that he no doubt intended to provoke insight are sometimes merely mystifying. Then there are the quotations. Like many another quotable author, Williams borrows at need. Ordinary quotations, introduced and cited as such, are not the problem. It is rather the unannounced echoes and references he weaves into his writing. He does it everywhere. Charitable readers may wish take it as a compliment, since he presumes a greater familiarity with a wider range of literature than most people are likely to have today. Phrases from the Authorized Version of Bible and the 1662 edition of the Book of Common Prayer are constantly being alluded to, but that is only the beginning. Even Lewis, who prided himself on being able to quote the gamut of English literature from memory, conceded that Williams did it far better. Only one of the essays included here is chiefly a piece of literary criticism, but Williams's knowledge of Wordsworth and Blake, Milton and Shakespeare, to say nothing of Dante, shows up at every turn. Moreover, although he was not a professional theologian he knew the vocabulary and was well acquainted with the standard authors, as well as some who are not so standard. Where an explanation or a translation seemed most needful it has been added, either as a note or within square brackets. Such devices are themselves distracting, however, and they are used sparingly. Otherwise the only changes that have been made affect spelling, capitalization, and the like, with one or two exceptions that are noted as they occur.

Something should be said about the order of this collection, which I have followed, roughly, in these introductory notes. It is not exactly a logical order, for two reasons. In the first place, many of the items collected here were originally independent, so that a certain amount of overlap could not be avoided. The rest come from books, and so were originally dependent—some more than others—on a context they lack here. Although I have tried to choose chapters that stand well on their own, they sometimes jostle their new neighbors. In certain cases, where the absence of any background makes itself felt most noticeably, I have tried to sketch it, either here or in a brief paragraph at the beginning.

Discontinuity and repetition are minor problems, however, and inevitable in an anthology. With Williams, a systematic order is out of the question for another reason. He was not a systematic thinker. A coherent thinker, yes, but not in the sense that he defined his terms and proceeded stepwise through a logical argument. He is certainly not illogical, but his logic is imaginative rather than linear. Several excellent studies, listed below, have been written by friends and scholars to present the whole of what can only be called Williams's vision, and it is worth noting that each of them follows a different sequence of topics and none manages to organize all Williams's ideas neatly. But is not their fault that something is always spilling over. Williams is like that.

Although I have said that Williams is not always an easy writer to read, neither this caution nor the exegetical apparatus should be taken to mean that he is pedantic or professorial. "You are the only writer since Dante," W.H. Auden told him, "who has found out how to make poetry out of theology and history." The reference is to Williams's verse, but in the prose collected here he does the same thing. The poetry he makes of theology and history in these essays will have its effect, as good poetry always does, on mind and feeling at once. The fare he offers is nourishing, if rich, and the time it takes to "inwardly digest" it will be time well spent.

SOURCES OF QUOTATIONS

(Unless otherwise noted, the author is Charles Williams. Quotations whose source is in this collection are not included.)

"if one is anxious to write about God": "The Productions of Time," *Time and Tide* 22 (25 January 1941) 72-73.

"whether that is or is not fiction": *The Descent of the Dove* (Grand Rapids: William B. Eerdmans, 1968), p. viii.

"beyond the resources of language": T. S. Eliot, introduction to *All Hallows Eve* (Grand Rapids: William B. Eerdmans, 1981), p. xi.

"All his books illuminate one another": Dorothy L. Sayers, "Dante and Charles Williams," in *Christian Letters to a Post-Christian World* (Grand Rapids: Eerdmans, 1969), p. 164.

"the frank supernaturalism and the frankly blood-curdling episodes": C. S. Lewis, preface to *Essays Presented to Charles Williams* (London: Oxford University Press, 1947), p. vii.

"I have never met any human being": E. Martin Browne, *Two in One* (Cambridge: Cambridge University Press, 1981), p. 101.

"The maze should be...exact": *He Came Down from Heaven* (Grand Rapids: Eerdmans, 1984), p. 39.

"the terms he deigns to apply": *Witchcraft* (New York: Meridian, 1959), p. 278.

"great humanist ode": *The Descent of the Dove*, p. 58.

"The mingled voices": *The Greater Trumps* (New York: Pellegrini & Cudahay, 1950), p. 125.

"immature and romantic devotions to the simple Jesus": *The Descent of the Dove*, p. 53.

"any human energy": *Outlines of Romantic Theology* (Grand Rapids: William B. Eerdmans, 1990), p. 9.

"that's exactly what Dante said!": Sayers, "Dante and Charles Williams," p. 163.

"the preference of an immediately satisfying experience": *He Came Down from Heaven*, pp. 42-43.

"the historical events...are a pageant": *He Came Down from Heaven*, p. 6.

"Romantic love between the sexes": *The Figure of Beatrice* (New York: Octagon Books, 1972), p. 63.

"was, in her degree": *The Figure of Beatrice*, p. 8.

CHARLES WILLIAMS

"There has been and is, now and always, only one question": *He Came Down from Heaven*, p. 89.

"Romantic love between the sexes": *The Figure of Beatrice*, p. 63.

"As a maxim for living": *The Descent of the Dove*, p. viii.

"Stanhope, turning his eyes": *Descent Into Hell* (Grand Rapids: William B. Eerdmans, 1970), pp. 100-101.

"the facts of present human existence": *He Came Down from Heaven*, p. 14.

"history is itself a myth": "The Figure of Arthur," in *Taliessin through Logres, The Region of the Summer Stars, and Arthurian Torso* (Grand Rapids: William B. Eerdmans, 1974), p. 264.

"Since there was not"; "They had what they wanted": *He Came Down from Heaven*, p. 19.

"Our bodies are innocent": *The Forgiveness of Sins* (Grand Rapids: William B. Eerdmans, 1984), p. 105.

"only two attitudes towards the sin of another": "Blake and Wordsworth," in *The Image of the City and Other Essays* (London: Oxford University Press, 1958), p. 66.

"the consciousness of repentance": *The Forgiveness of Sins*, p. 57.

"forgave? say he loved": *The Forgiveness of Sins*, p. 64.

"Christianity and life ought to be one": *The Forgiveness of Sins*, p. 70.

"as broad as creation": *The Descent of the Dove*, p. 128.

"You are the only writer since Dante": quoted by Glen Cavaliero in *Charles Williams: Poet of Theology* (Grand Rapids: William B. Eerdmans, 1983), p. 171.

SOME STUDIES OF CHARLES WILLIAMS

Auden W.H. "Charles Williams." *Christian Century* 73 (2 May 1956) 552-554.

Carpenter, Humphrey. *The Inklings.* London: George Allen & Unwin, 1978.

Cavaliero, Glen. *Charles Williams: Poet of Theology.* Grand Rapids: William B. Eerdmans, 1983.

Hadfield, Mary Alice. *Charles Williams: An Exploration of His Life and Work.* Oxford University Press, 1983.

Hillegas, Mark R. (ed.). *Shadows of Imagination: The Fantasies of C.S. Lewis, J.R.R. Tolkien, and Charles Williams.* Carbondale: Southern Illinois University Press, 1969.

Howard, Thomas. *The Novels of Charles Williams.* Oxford University Press, 1983.

Ridler, Anne. "Introduction." In *The Image of the City and Other Essays,* by Charles Williams. Oxford University Press, 1958.

Shideler, Mary McDermott. *The Theology of Romantic Love: A Study in the Writings of Charles Williams.* New York: Harper & Brothers, 1962.

Sibley, Agnes. *Charles Williams.* Boston: Twayne Publishers, 1982.

Walsh, Chad. "Charles Williams's Novels and the Contemporary Mutation of Consciousness." In *Myth, Allegory, and Gospel,* ed. John Warwick Montgomery. Minneapolis: Bethany Fellowship, 1974.

NATURAL GOODNESS

This essay, written not long after *He Came Down from Heaven* and while Williams was at work on *The Forgiveness of Sins*, offers an overview of the theological outlook those books elaborate. It was published in *Theology*, October 1941.

I t is a little unfortunate that in ordinary English talk the words "natural" and "supernatural" have come to be considered as opposed rather than as complementary. Something like it has happened with those other words "nature" and "grace," but less frequently, since the second two are more often used by trained theologians. But certainly the common use of the first two words implies rather a division between their meanings than a union.

This would be more comprehensible if we meant by "supernatural" only the world of angels and of God. It is true that God is so wholly "other" that only in the broadest sense can anything we mean by "supernatural" be applied to him any more than "natural." But of the two terms we must use one rather than the other. And the forces of the world of angels are certainly different from our own "natural" forces. It is also true that the Christian religion has asserted that those "natural" forces are but elements, and even infinitesimal elements, in the whole range of creation. But they are so far harmonious with it that they appear contrary only because of that element in man which we call sin, and they are not insignificant or negligible. The "supernatural" must therefore in some sense include the "natural." "A new earth" was promised as well as "a new heaven." Whatever the promise means, that earth is presumably in some relation to this earth.

Matter, certainly, is by definition the opposite of spirit. It is apparently as far the opposite of God (leaving will and morals out of the question) as God chose to create. But it did not therefore become less significant of him than that less technical opposite which is called spirit. We have, in fact, only lost proper comprehension of matter by an apostasy in spirit. Matter and "nature" have not, in themselves, sinned; what has sinned is spirit, if spirit and matter are to be regarded as divided. That they so easily can be is due perhaps to that lack of intellectual clarity produced by the Fall.

There is, I understand, an opinion permissible to the faithful which may be discussed here. I am told that it is related to the great name of Duns Scotus, and no doubt it is, if permissible, familiar to readers of *Theology*. But it is illuminating on this subject and illustrates the problem of natural goodness.

It is, briefly, that the Incarnation is the point of creation, and the divine "reason" for it. It pleased God in his self-willed activity to be incarnate. But obviously this union of himself with matter in flesh did not necessarily involve the creation of other flesh. It would have been sufficient to himself to be himself united with matter, and that "united with" means a union very much beyond our powers to conceive; more than a union, a unity. Even now, in spite of the Athanasian Creed, the single existence of the Incarnate Word is too often almost gnostically contemplated as an inhabitation of the flesh by the Word. But it is not so; what he is, he is wholly and absolutely, and even in his death and in the separation of body and soul he remains wholly and absolutely one. His act could have been to himself alone. He decreed that it should not be; he determined creation; he determined not only to be incarnate, but to be incarnate by means of a mother. He proposed to himself to be born into a world.

This decree upon himself was the decree that brought mankind into being. It was his will to make creatures of such a kind that they should share in that particular joy of his existence in flesh. He bade for himself a mother and all her companions; perhaps the mystery of the mortal maternity of God was greater even than that, but at least it was that. It was the great and single act of active love, consonant with nothing but his nature, compared to which the Redemption (if indeed he were infinitely to maintain all souls alive) was but a sheer act of justice. Our flesh was to hold, to its degree, the secrets of his own.

Nothing has ever altered, nothing could ever alter, that decree. I do not, of course, mean even to seem to separate it from his other acts; only one must speak in terms of time. Certainly he acted altogether, he created and redeemed and judged and executed judgment all at once. But it seems that, as far as we are concerned, he also in that act created process and therefore time, time being in this sense the mere measurement of process. Indeed, so determining to be incarnate by a mother, it might perhaps be said that he determined process for himself also, and even that, for pure increase of joy, he determined that the process should depend on the freewill of his mother and of men. He designed exchange of joy; he gave us the final privilege of owing everything to ourselves as well as to him. This moment was our primal nature, and nothing has ever altered that fact—not though we may wish it had.

There followed, as we know, the chosen catastrophe which we call the Fall. Whether in that state in which mankind was, the Fall was a single act of a single soul, or the simultaneous act of all souls, this is not the place to discuss. It is, I suppose, possible (since it is to be believed that every human creature sins) that in some way every human nature sinned at once; that the whole web was at once and everywhere ruined. That is irrelevant to the fact that, however it happened, it certainly happened. The will of man sinned. But the will of man was a spiritual quality; it was in his soul. It was that power in him which we call the soul that sinned. It was not the power which we call the flesh. It was therefore the "supernatural" which sinned. The "natural," as we now call it, did not. They cannot, of course, be separated. But if, in terminology, they can be, then it is the matter of our substance which has remained faithful, and the immaterial which has not.

The definition of the Fall is that man determined to know good as evil. Whether (as may be) it was indeed an affair of the fruit of a tree or whether that is symbolical does not matter. But if the good, which was whole, was to be known as evil, then process must be known as evil; that is, the process must be to a living death. The end would be hell. But all the qualities and all the glories of that human creation were not in one moment changed to a state of hell. So much the decree of process itself forbade. The end might be inevitable, but it had to be gradual.

His nature, as it were, was still implanted in his creatures; it was, indeed, human for divine, their nature. Nor has that foundation ever failed. They devoted it to everlasting death. But the genius of it, so to speak, was of eternal life. He who had desired his creatures to accept his choice now accepted the terms of his creation; he accepted the choice of his creatures. The Incarnation became also the Redemption. He became the new thing. But that did not prevent him from being the foundation of the old thing. He was, is, and is to be, the light that lighteneth every man.

The apostolic and catholic faith declared the Redemption of fallen nature, but that Redemption was on the principles and to the principles of our first unfallen nature. Man could not longer be innocent; he was corrupt, and his best efforts were, but for the new grace, doomed to death. But his best efforts were, and are, of no other kind than had been decreed. His blood might be tainted, but the source from which it sprang was still the same. His natural life was still, and is now, a disordered pattern of the only pattern, a confused type of the one original; it is full still of glory and of peace, as well as of bloodshed and despair. It contends within itself. The most extreme goodness may be found in it and asserted of it— so long as the absolute invalidity of it apart from the new life is also declared. The most absolute domination of the new life may be asserted, so long as the accidental goodness of the old is never denied.

It is no doubt true that the operations of the Christian church for two thousand years—sacramental, doctrinal, and moral—have had a greater effect than we generally realize. When all allowances, however, have been made for this, and for the various legal and social systems which, touched by Christianity as well as by civic security, have faintly aimed at goodness, it remains true that the goodness in the "natural" order often seems to rival and equal the goodness of the "supernatural." Something very much like heroic sanctity exists everywhere. This heroic sanctity outside the Christian church is a thing for which Christians are always "making allowances." I use the silly phrase because it is the only one that fits. They do not, perhaps, mean it to sound so; the effect is due to the use of a great vocabulary by inadequate voices. It is also due to the unintentionally insincere claims made by foolish Christians on behalf of their Christian experience. Vigil, heroism, martyrdom, vicarious life, are common to man. In so far as they are possible outside the church, they are elements of man's original nature operative within him in spite of, but under conditions of, the catastrophe of the Fall. In so far as they are impossible inside the church, they are the change in man's fallen nature which even grace has not yet renewed. Nature and grace are categories of one Identity.

What, then, are we to hold is the value of the Christian religion? It is applicable far beyond itself, in the sense that what it says is the only final validity of those other great acts of goodness. Union with our sacred Lord is obtained by acts. Belief is, no doubt, an act; proper motive is an act; but also an act is an act. The great doctrines are the only explanation and the only hope. But even the great doctrines are only the statement of something as wide as the universe and as deep as the human heart. They do not deny as Creator that which they adore as Savior, though the Creator had to become a Savior lest his creation should be wholly lost. It is to be believed that, except by the cross and resurrection, no act is valid; and that by that cross and resurrection the proper validity of every act is determined. The Christian church has been charged with the great secrets which are the only facts of existence. But the visible and vocal church will have to practice much humility, in itself as well as in its separate members, before it can find itself capable of speaking on equal terms with that nature which it has to regenerate with universal blessing.

The Incarnation of the Son of God led to the cross because it summed up and prevented the otherwise inevitable end of human process both individual and general. But it is at least a question whether the Incarnation only existed to lead to the cross or whether it was in fact the original act. The church is the means of penitence and faith. But the lack of penitence and faith cannot altogether destroy the value of what remains of natural goodness. The transformation of natural goodness into eternal goodness demands all stress on both the Incarnation and the crucifixion. Our great difficulty is that it is much easier to transform eternal goodness, or what should be eternal goodness, into natural goodness. "When religion is in the hands of the natural man," wrote William Law, "he is always the worse for it; it adds a bad heat to his own dark fire and helps to inflame his four elements of selfishness, envy, pride and wrath." But it was the same William Law who wrote:

> Natural religion, if you understand it rightly, is a most excellent thing, it is a right sentiment of heart, it is so much goodness in the heart, it is its sensibility both of its separation from and its relation to God; and therefore it shows itself in nothing but in a penitential sentiment of the weight of its sins, and in an humble recourse by faith to the mercy of God. Call but this the religion of nature and then the more you esteem it, the better; for you cannot wish well to it without bringing it to the Gospel state of perfection. For the religion of the Gospel is this religion of penitence and faith in the mercy of God, brought forth into its full perfection. For the Gospel calls you to nothing but to know and understand and practise a full and real penitence, and to know by faith such heights and depths of the divine mercy towards you, as the religion of nature had only some little uncertain glimmerings of.

Remove the word "God" from that description of natural religion, remove the word "religion," and the principles still hold. Those principles are in our nature because of his, and the Word (and we by the Word) are other than all the vocabularies.

THE INCARNATION OF THE KINGDOM

At the beginning of *He Came Down from Heaven* Williams says that for "those of us who are neither theologians, higher critics, nor fundamentalists" what is needed in order to understand the Bible is first of all good literary criticism. In this chapter, originally entitled "The Precursor and the Incarnation of the Kingdom," he supplies that need in respect of the gospels.

The earliest of the gospels is asserted to be that called "of Mark"; it is certainly the shortest. As Genesis had explained what was happening by what had happened, so do the gospels. They purport to be a record of the cause of certain definite experiences. The time and place of that cause are definitely marked. It occurs in certain named towns of the Roman Empire, in a period from 4 B.C. to A.D. 30, from forty to seventy years after the death of Julius Caesar, and from fifteen to fifty years after the death of Virgil. The administration of the imperial government organizes everything, and the events are plotted along the lines of that organization. The *pietas* of the early and mythical wanderers has become a supernatural civilization. The documents of the New Testament are themselves composed in or directed to localities in that interrelated whole, and before it is well understood what the church is, it is at least clear that it is universal. At the same time, history and contemporaneity again go together, the obverse and the reverse of the coins of the kingdom of heaven. Its missionaries declared a unity, as they do today, a unity no more divided by two thousand years than by two seconds. We certainly have to separate them in thought, because of the needs of the mind, as we have sometimes to divide form and content in poetry. But as the poetry is in fact one and indivisible, so is the fact; so even is the doctrine. The thing as it happens on the earth and in the world, the thing as it happens on the earth and in the soul, are two stresses on one fact; say, on one Word. The fact is the thing that is supposed to have appeared, and the gospel of Mark is the shortest account. The gospels called "of Matthew" and "of Luke" are longer and fuller. The gospel called "of John" comes nearer to describing the unity of the new thing in world and soul; it is the limit of the permissible influence of contemporary Greek philosophy, and the repulse of the impermissible. To observe something of the distinction one has only to consider the *Symposium* of Plato with the gospel of John, and remark the difference in their attitude towards matter.

It is asserted that the gospel according to Mark was in circulation at Rome by the year 75. If so, and if the gospel of Mark represents at all what the church believed or tried to believe in the year 75, then certainly by the year 75 the church at the center of a highly developed society had already thrown over any idea (if any such idea had ever existed) of a figure only of brotherly love and international peace; the moral teacher expanding the old Jewish ideas of pardon and righteousness into a fresh beauty, and teaching ethics in the ancient maxim of the Golden Rule. Possibly a figure of this kind might be extracted from Saint John's gospel, by leaving out rather more than half of Saint John's gospel. But with the gospel of Saint Mark the thing is impossible. To remove the apocalyptic is not to leave the ethical but to leave nothing at all.

It is, of course, arguable that the influence of Saint Paul, who is often regarded as the villain of early Christianity (the Claudius of a *Hamlet* from which Hamlet has been removed), had already had its perfect work. Or, since there had not been very much time for Saint Paul to do it, perhaps someone earlier, an Ur-Paul, or (documentarily) the fatal and fascinating Q which no man has seen at any time but the contents of which we so neatly know. The weakness, credulity, and folly of that early disciple, or of all the early disciples, may have altered the original truth of the vagrant provincial professor of ethical beauty into something more closely corresponding to their romantic needs. Saint Mark may be dogmatically asserted to have been an intentional or unintentional liar. But at least we have to admit his lies for the purpose of explaining that they are lies. They are our only evidence for whatever it was he was lying about. And as he was not lying in a sub-prefecture of Thule, but right in the middle of the Empire, so he was not lying about events older than the dynasties of Egypt or the cities of Assyria, but about events done on a hill outside a city on a Roman highway under the rule of the Princeps Augustus and his successor Tiberius. They were (in one sense or the other—or both) historic lies.

Our contemporary pseudo-acquaintance with the Christian idea has misled us in another point. It is generally supposed that his lies (if lies) are simple and easy. It is only by reading Saint Mark that one discovers they are by no means simple or easy. It is very difficult to make out what is supposed to be happening. His book begins with a declaration: "The beginning of the gospel of Jesus Christ, the Son of God." What the

Son of God may be he does not explain, preferring to follow it up with a quotation from the old prophets which slides into an account of a certain John who came as the precursor of this divine Hero. He has in Saint Mark no other business, and this (though highly wrought to a fine passion of declamation and heraldry) is so in Saint John. But in Saint Luke there is something more. It is recorded that certain groups came to the Precursor—the common people, the tax-collectors, the soldiers. All these ask him for some kind of direction on conduct. Saint Matthew adds the ecclesiastical leaders, but the Precursor offered them no more than invective. He answers the rest with instructions which amount very nearly to a gospel of temporal justice. All men are to share their goods freely and equally. The revenue officers are to make no personal profit out of their business. The soldiers are not to make their duties an excuse for outrage or violence; they (again) are to make no personal gain beyond their government pay. Share everything; neither by fraud nor by force let yourself be unfair to anyone; be content with your own proper pay. It is true he does not raise the question of the restoration of the dispossessed by force of arms; he is speaking of immediate duties as between individual and individual. "He that hath two coats let him give to him that hath none." He prolongs the concern of the prophets with social injustice, without their denunciation of the proud. That had been declared, as a duty of the imperial government, by the great poet dead forty five years before:

> *Pacisque imponere morem,*
> *Parcere subiectis et debellare superbos:*

"To impose the habit of peace, to be merciful to the downtrodden, and to overthrow the proud." There had been a similar note in the private song (again according to Saint Luke) of the Mother of the coming Hero: "the rich he hath sent empty away."

At this moment the Divine Thing appears (it will be remembered that Saint Matthew uses the neuter—"that holy *thing*"; students of the gospel may be excused for sometimes following the example, if only to remind ourselves of what the evangelists actually said). In the rest of Saint Mark's first chapter, the account of his coming is purely apocalyptic. Witness is borne out of heaven and on earth and from hell. He (since the masculine pronoun is also and more frequently used) begins his own activities. He calls disciples; he works miracles of healing; he controls spirits; he teaches with authority. What does he teach? what do the devils fear and the celestials declare and men wonder at? "The time is fulfilled, and the kingdom of God is at hand; repent ye and believe the gospel."

Yes, but what gospel? what kind of kingdom? The Precursor had said almost the same thing. In some expectation one turns the page...several pages. The works of healing continue swiftly, interspersed with the Divine Thing's comments on himself, and his reasons for existing. They are still not very clear. The old prophetic cry of "pardon" returns. He has power to forgive sins—does he mean forget? He calls himself the "Son of Man"; he is lord of ritual observances such as the keeping of the Sabbath; there exists some state of eternal sin and damnation. There is something—presumably the kingdom of heaven—which cannot be reconciled with old things; new, it must be fitted to the new.

Presently, in the parables, the description of the kingdom is continued. It is a state of being, but not a state of being without which one can get along very well. To lose it is to lose everything else. It is intensely dangerous, and yet easily neglected. It involves repentance and it involves "faith"—whatever "faith" may be. It is concerned with himself, for he attributes to himself the power and the glory. He says: "I say unto thee, Arise"; "it is I; be not afraid." The Sermon on the Mount is full of his own decisions, just as it ramps with hell and destruction and hypocrites and being cast into the fire and trodden under foot and demands for perfection and for joy (not for resignation or endurance or forgiveness, not even a pseudo-joy) under intolerable treatment. Moses in old days had momentarily taken the power and the glory to himself, and had been shut out of the temporal promise. But the present Hero does it continuously, until (in the topmost note of that exalted arrogance) humility itself is vaunted, and the only virtue that cannot be aware of itself without losing its nature is declared by the Divine Thing to be its own nature: "I am meek and lowly of heart." This in the voice that says to the Syrophoenician woman when she begs help for her daughter: "It is not meet to take the children's bread, and to cast it unto the dogs." It is true her request is granted, in answer to her retort, something in the same manner as the Lord spoke to Job in answer to his.

About halfway through the book as we have it, there is a change. Up to chapter 8 it is possible to believe that, though the doctrine is anything but clear, the experience of the disciples is not unique. Figures are sometimes met who overwhelm, frighten, and delight those who come in contact with them; personality, and so forth—and what they say may easily sound obscure. But in chapter 8 there is a sudden concentration and even exposition. The Hero demands from his disciples a statement, not of their repentance or righteousness or belief in the I AM, which is what the old prophets clamored for, but of their belief in himself, and he follows it up with a statement of his own.

They say: "Thou art the Christ." No doubt when we have looked up annotated editions and biblical dictionaries, we know what "the Christ" means. It is "the Anointed One." But at the moment, there, it is a kind of incantation, the invocation of a ritual, antique, and magical title. Even if we look up the other gospels and make it read: "Thou art the Christ, the Son of the living God," it does not much help. However inspired Saint Peter may have been, it seems unlikely that he comprehended in a flash the whole complex business of Christian theology. What is the Son of God? The apostles and the devils agree; that is something. But on what do they agree?

The Divine Thing approves the salutation. It proceeds to define its destiny. It declares it is to suffer greatly, to be rejected by all the centers of jurisdiction, to be seized and put to death, and after three days it is to rise again from the dead. Protests are abusively tossed aside. In all three gospels this definition of its immediate future is followed by a definition of its further nature and future; "the Son of Man" is to be seen in the "glory of his Father and with the holy angels," that is, in the swift and geometrical glory seen by Isaiah and Ezekiel, the fire of the wheels and the flash of the living creatures, the terrible crystal and the prism of the covenant above, the pattern of heaven declared in heaven. The formula of the knowledge of this pattern on earth is disclosed; it is the loss of life for the saving of life, "for my sake and the gospel's." It is the denial of the self and the lifting of the cross.

The denial of the self has come, as is natural, to mean in general the making of the self thoroughly uncomfortable. That (though it may be all that is possible) leaves the self still strongly existing. But the phrase is more intellectual than moral, or rather it is only moral because it is intellectual; it is a denial of the consciousness of the existence of the self at all. What had been the self is to become a single individual, neither less nor more than others; as it were, one of the living creatures that run about and compose the web of the glory. "Do unto others as you would they should do unto you." The contemplation demanded is not personal, of the self and of others—even in order that the self may be unselfish—but abstract and impartial. The life of the self is to be lost that the individual soul may be found, in the pattern of the words of the Son of Man. The kingdom is immediately at hand—"Verily I say unto you, That there be some of them that stand here, which shall not taste of death, till they have seen the kingdom of God come with power"; again the words are historic and contemporary at once.

The declaration of the formula is followed by what is called the Transfiguration. Secluded among a few of his followers, the Divine Thing exhibits itself in a sudden brightness, in which, as if it receded into the eternal state of contemporaneousness, the ancient leaders of what had once been the inclusive-exclusive covenant of salvation are discerned to exchange speech with the new exclusive figure of inclusive beatitude. It is a vision which is to be kept a secret till the rising from the dead has been accomplished. But at least the kingdom has now been, to some extent, exhibited. Repentance is a preliminary to the denial of the self and the loss of the life, and the loss of the life for the saving of the life depends on that choosing of necessity by the Son of Man which will take him to his death and rising. "He set his face to go up to Jerusalem."

It is at some time during this period of the operation of the Christ that the problem of the Precursor reappears. Messengers from John arrive; "art thou he that was to come?" After they have been dismissed, the Christ, turning to those that stood by (as it were to his mother and to his brethren), makes the astonishing declaration that "among men born of women is none greater than John the Baptist, yet the least in the kingdom of heaven is greater than he." The church since then has implied that this can hardly be true in its literal sense, for the Precursor has been canonized (as it were, by acclamation) and been given a feast to himself, a Primary Double of the

First Class.[1] Even so, even assuming that as a matter of fact the Precursor was and is one of the greatest in the kingdom of heaven, still the Christ must have had something in his mind. What, apart from the expectation of the Redeemer, was the gospel of the Precursor? It was something like complete equality and temporal justice, regarded as the duty of those who expect the kingdom. What has happened to that duty in the gospel of the kingdom?

The new gospel does not care much about it. All John's doctrine is less than the least in the kingdom. It cannot be bothered with telling people not to defraud and not to be violent and to share their superfluities. It tosses all that sort of thing on one side. Let the man who has two coats (said the Precursor) give one to the man who has none. But what if the man who has none, or for that matter the man who has three, wants to take one from the man who has two—what then? Grace of heaven! why, give him both. If a man has stolen the pearl bracelet, why, point out to him that he has missed the diamond necklace. Be content with your wages, said the Precursor. The Holy Thing decorated that advice with a suggestion that it is iniquity to be displeased when others who have done about a tenth as much work are paid as much money: "is thine eye evil because mine is good?" It is true that there is a reason—those who came in late had not been hired early. No one would accept that as a reason today—neither economist nor employer nor worker. But there is always a reason; the intellectual logic of the prophets is carried on into the New Testament. Yet the separate and suitable reasons never quite account for the identical and indivisible command. The "sweet reasonableness" of Christ is always there, but it is always in a dance and its dancing-hall is from the topless heavens to the bottomless abyss. Its balance is wholly in itself; it is philosophical and unconditioned by temporalities—"had, having, and in quest to have, extreme."

Half a hundred brief comments, flung out to the mob of men's hearts, make it impossible for a child of the kingdom, for a Christian, to talk of justice or injustice so far as he personally is concerned; they make it impossible for him to *complain* of the unfairness of anything. They do not, presumably, stop him noticing what has happened, but it can never be a matter of protest. Judgment and measurement are always discouraged. You may have them if you will, but there is a sinister note in the promise that they shall be measured back to you in the same manner: "good measure, pressed down and running over shall men give into your bosoms." If you must have law, have it, "till thou hast paid the uttermost farthing."

What then of all the great tradition, the freeing of slaves at the Exodus, the determination of the prophets, the long effort against the monstrous impiety of Cain? The answer is obvious; all that is assumed as a mere preliminary. The rich, while they remain rich, are practically incapable of salvation, at which all the apostles were exceedingly astonished. Their astonishment is exceedingly funny to our vicariously generous minds. But if riches are not supposed to be confined to money, the astonishment becomes more general. There are many who feel that while God might damn Rothschild he could hardly damn Rembrandt. Are the riches of Catullus and Carnegie so unequal, though so different? Sooner or later, nearly everyone is surprised at some kind of rich man being damned.

The Divine Thing, for once, was tender to us; he restored a faint hope: "with God all things are possible." But the preliminary step is always assumed: "sell all that thou hast and give it to the poor"—and then we will talk. Then we will talk of that other thing without which even giving to the poor is useless, the thing for which at another time the precious ointment was reserved from the poor, the thing that is necessary to correct and qualify even good deeds, the thing that is formulated in the words "for my sake and the gospel's" or "in my name." Good deeds are not enough; even love is not enough unless it is love of a particular kind. Long afterwards Saint Paul caught up the dreadful cry: "though I bestow all my goods to feed the poor...and have not charity, it profiteth me nothing." It is not surprising that Messias saw the possibility of an infinitely greater knowledge of evil existing through him than had been before: "blessed is he whosoever shall not be offended at me."

The Incarnation of the kingdom has declared its destiny, the formula by which man may be unified with it, the preliminaries necessary to the spiritual initiation. The records of the synoptic gospels proceed to the awful and familiar tale: to the entry of the Divine Thing into Jerusalem, to its making of itself a substance of communication through the flesh, to its passion. "The Son of Man is betrayed into the hands of sinners." In the ancient myth something of that kind had happened to the good, the good in which the Adam had lived. But that good had not, in the myth, been imagined as a consciousness. The kingdom of heaven then had not been shown as affected by the sin of the Adam; only the Adam. The patience which had been proclaimed in the covenants had been the self-restraint of the Creator, but not—there—of the Victim. Another side of the aeonian process has issued slowly into knowledge; the operation of that in the Adam and in their descendants which had remained everlastingly related to the good.

The gospel called "of John" begins with that original. The Divine Thing is there identified with the knowledge of good which indefectibly exists in every man—indefectibly even though it should be experienced only as hell—"the light which lighteth every man." It is also that by which communication with the heaven of perfection is maintained, "ascending and descending." But this state of being which is called "the kingdom of heaven" in the synoptics is called in Saint John "eternal life." There is no space here to work out singly the various definitions of itself which it provides in this gospel. Briefly, it declares itself to be the union of heaven and earth (1:51); the one absolutely necessary thing for escape from a state in which the contradiction of good is preferred (3:16, 36); it is the perfect satisfaction of desire (6:35; 10:27-28); it is judgment (5:25-30; 12:46-48); it is in perfect union with its Origin (10:30; 14:11); it is universal and inclusive (15:5; 17:21); it restores the truth (5:33; 7:31-32; 18:37). Of these the last is perhaps the most related to the present argument. For by truth must be meant at least perfect knowledge (within the proper requisite degrees). "Ye shall know the truth, and the truth shall make you free." Right knowledge and freedom are to be one.

It is this "truth" of which the Divine Hero speaks at the time of the passion which he had prophesied—as necessity and as his free choice. Before one of the jurisdictions by which he is rejected and condemned he declares: "To this end was I born, and for this cause came I into the world, that I should bear witness unto the truth. Everyone that is of the truth heareth my voice." He formally claimed before another the ritual titles of Son of God and Son of Man, and his future descent "in the clouds of heaven" and in the glory of heaven. But before then the earlier proclamation, "the kingdom of heaven is at hand," has changed. It has become concentrated; if the kingdom, then the moment of the arrival of the kingdom. The gospels break into peremptory phrases: "My time is at hand," "this night," "this hour"; an image of the hour absorbed into the Holy Thing is thrown up—"this cup"; the hour arrives—"behold, the Son of Man is betrayed into the hands of sinners."

Around that moment the world of order and judgment, of Virgil and the Precursor, of Pharaoh and Cain, rushes up also. Its good and its evil are both concerned, for it cannot very well do other than it does do. The knowledge of good as evil has made the whole good evil to it; it has to reject the good in order to follow all that it can understand as good. When Caiaphas said that "it was good that one man should die for the people," he laid down a principle which every government supports and must support. Nor, though Christ has denounced the government for its other sins, does he denounce either Caiaphas or Pilate for his own death. He answers the priest; he condescends to discussion with the Roman. Only to Herod he says nothing, for Herod desired neither the ecclesiastical nor the political good; he wanted only miracles to amuse him. The miracles of Christ are accidental, however efficient; the kingdom of heaven fulfills all earthly laws because that is its nature but it is concerned only with its own, and to try to use it for earth is to lose heaven and gain nothing for earth. It may be taken by violence but it cannot be compelled by violence; its Incarnation commanded that he should be awaited everywhere but his effectiveness demanded nowhere. Everything must be made ready and then he will do what he likes. This maxim, which is the condition of all prayer, has involved the church in a metaphysics of prayer equivalent to "Heads, I win; tails, you lose."

The three jurisdictions acted according to all they could understand of good: Caiaphas upon all he could know of the religious law, Pilate of the Virgilian equity, Herod of personal desire. The Messias answered them in that first word of the cross which entreated pardon for them precisely on the ground of their ignorance: "forgive them, for they know not what they do." The knowledge of good and evil which man had desired is offered as the excuse for their false knowledge of good. But the offer brings their false knowledge into consciousness, and will no longer like the prophets blot it out.

The new way of pardon is to be different from the old, for the evil is still to be known.

It is known, in what follows, by the Thing that has come down from Heaven. He experiences a complete and utter deprivation of all knowledge of the good. The church has never defined the Atonement. It has contented itself with saying that the Person of the kingdom there assumed into itself the utmost possible capacities of its own destruction and they could not destroy it. It separated itself from all good deliberately and (as it were) superfluously: "thinkest thou I cannot now pray to the Father and he shall presently give me more than twelve legions of angels? But how then shall the scriptures be fulfilled, that thus it must be?" It could, it seems, still guiltlessly free itself, but it has made its own promise and will keep it. Its impotency is deliberate. It denies its self; it loses its life to save it; it saves others because it cannot, by its decisions, save itself. It remains still exclusive and inclusive; it excludes all consent to the knowledge of evil, but it includes the whole knowledge of evil without its own consent. It is "made sin," in Saint Paul's phrase. The prophecy quoted concerning this paradox of redemption is "A bone of him shall not be broken," and this is fulfilled; as if the frame of the universe remains entire, but its life is drawn out of it, as if the pattern of the glory remained exact but the glory itself were drawn away.

The height of the process begins with the agony in the garden, which is often quoted for our encouragement; he shuddered and shrank. The shrinking is part of the necessity; he "must" lose power; he "must" know fear. He "must" be like the Adam in the garden of the myth, only where they fled from their fear into the trees he goes among the trees to find his fear; he is secluded into terror. The process reaches its height, after from the cross he has still asserted the *pietas*, the exchanged human responsibility, of men: "behold thy son, behold thy mother," and after he has still declared the pure dogma of his nature, known now as hardly more than dogma: "today thou shalt be with me in Paradise." This is what he has chosen, and as his power leaves him he still chooses, to believe. He becomes, but for that belief, a state wholly abandoned.

Gibbon, in that superb as well as solemn sneer which is one of the classic pages of English prose as well as one of the supreme attacks on the whole history, may have been right. The whole earth may not have been darkened, nor even the whole land. Pliny and Seneca may have recorded no wonder because there was no wonder to record. The sun may have seemed to shine on Calvary as on many another more protracted agony. Or there may have been a local eclipse, or whatever other phenomenon the romantic pietists can invent to reconcile themselves to the other side. But that the life of the whole of mankind began to fail in that hour is not incredible; that the sun and all light, without as within, darkened before men's eyes, that the swoon of something more than death touched them, and its sweat stood on their foreheads to the farthest ends of the world. The Thing that was, and had always been, and must always be; the fundamental humanity of all men; the Thing that was man rather than a man, though certainly incarnated into the physical appearance of a man; the Thing that was Christ Jesus, knew all things in the deprivation of all goodness.

The darkness passed; men went on their affairs. He said: "It is finished." The passion and the resurrection have been necessarily divided in ritual and we think of them as separate events. So certainly they were, and yet not as separate as all that. They are two operations in one; they are the hour of the coming of the kingdom. A new knowledge arises. Men had determined to know good as evil; there could be but one perfect remedy for that—to know the evil of the past itself as good,

and to be free from the necessity of the knowledge of evil in
the future; to find right knowledge and perfect freedom together; to know all things as occasions of love. The Adam and
their children had been involved in a state of contradiction
within themselves. The law had done its best by imposing on
that chaos of contradiction a kind of order, by at least calling
definite things good and definite things evil. The prophets
had urged this method: repent, "cease to do evil, learn to do
well." But even allowing that, in all times and places, it was
possible to know what was good and what was evil, was it as
easy as all that? Or what of Job who had done well and was
overthrown? Or Ecclesiastes who had sought out righteousness and found it was all much the same vanity in the end?
How could the single knowledge be restored? Or if the myth
itself were false, how could the single knowledge be gained—
the knowledge of perfection in all experience which man
naturally desires and naturally believes, and as naturally denies and contradicts?

The writings of the early masters of the new life, the life
that was declared after the resurrection, are full of an awful
simplicity. The thing has happened; the kingdom is here.
"Fear not, little flock," wrote one of them, "it is your Father's
good pleasure to give you the kingdom." "What shall deliver
me," wrote another, "from the body of this death? I thank
God, through Jesus Christ our Lord." This clarity of knowledge rides through the epistles. All is most well; evil is "pardoned"—it is known after another manner; in an interchange
of love, as a means of love, therefore as a means of the good.
O felix culpa[2]—pardon is no longer an oblivion but an increased knowledge, a knowledge of all things in a perfection
of joy.

It is the name now given to the heavenly knowledge of the
evil of earth; evil is known as an occasion of good, that is, of
love. It has been always so known on the side of heaven, but

now it can be so known on the side of earth also. Pardon, or reconciliation, was not defined by the prophets as more than oblivion, for in time mankind had not experienced that reconciliation. Nor could mankind, by itself, ever reach it, for mankind by itself could not endure the results of its choice, the total deprivation of good, and yet recover joyous awareness of good. What mankind could not do, manhood did, and a manhood which was at the disposal of all men and women. It was therefore possible now for mankind itself to know evil as an occasion of heavenly love. It was not inappropriate that the condition of such a pardon should be repentance, for repentance is no more than a passionate intention to know all things after the mode of heaven, and it is impossible to know evil as good if you insist on knowing it as evil.

Pardon, as between any two beings, is a reidentification of love, and it is known so in the most tender and the most happy human relationships. But there is a profound difference between any such reidentification of love between heaven and earth and between earth and earth. What may be justly required in the one case must not be required in the other. It is all very well for the Divine Thing of heaven to require some kind of intention of good, not exactly as a condition of pardon but as a means of the existence of its perfection. Men were never meant to be as gods or to know as gods, and for men to make any such intention a part of their pardon is precisely to try to behave as gods. It is the renewal of the first and most dreadful error, the desire to know as gods; the reversal of the Incarnation, by which God knew as man, the heresy of thought and action denounced in the Athanasian Creed—it is precisely the attempt to convert the Godhead into flesh and not the taking of the manhood into God.

The intention to do differently may be passionately offered; it must never be required—not in the most secret recesses of that self which can only blush with shame to find itself pardoning and with delight at the infinite laughter of the universe at a created being forgiving another created being. The ancient cry of "Don't do it again" is never a part of pardon. It is conceivable that Saint Peter reidentified love between himself and his brother four hundred and ninety times in a day; it is inconceivable that each time he made it a condition of love that it shouldn't happen again—it would be a slur on intelligence as well as love. To consent to know evil as good only on condition that the evil never happens again is silly; it is conditioning one's knowledge—as if one consented to know that the Antipodes existed only on condition that no one ever mentioned the Antipodes. All limitation of pardon must come, if at all, from the side of the sinner, in the frequent cry of "I won't do it again," in the more frequent cry of "I won't, but I shall...." Heaven has had to explain to us not only itself but ourselves; it has had to create for us not only pardon but the nature of the desire for pardon. It has therefore defined the cry of the sinner, but it has not suggested that other sinners should take upon themselves to demand the cry before they submit, with their brothers, to its single glorious existence in both.

He rose; he manifested; he talked of "the things pertaining to the kingdom." He exhibited the actuality of his body, carrying the lovely and adorable matter, with which all souls were everlastingly conjoined, into his eternity. He left one great commandment—satisfy hunger: "feed the lambs," "feed the sheep." Beyond the Petrine law he cast the Johannine—"if I will that he tarry till I come..." but the coming may be from moment to moment and the tarrying from moment to moment. "Jesus said not unto him, He shall not die; but, If I will that he tarry till I come, what is that to thee?" It is as if, from moment to moment, he withdrew and returned, swifter than lightning, known in one mode and another mode and always new. The new life might still be sequential (in the order of time) but every instant was united to the Origin, and complete and absolute in itself. "Behold, I come quickly"—the coming and the going one, the going and the coming one, and all is joy. "It is not for you to know the times and the seasons...but you shall be witnesses to me..to the uttermost ends of the earth," through all the distances and all the operations of holy matter.

Then, as if it withdrew into the air within the air, and the air became a cloud about its passage, scattering promises of power, the Divine Thing parted and passed.

Endnotes

1. In older church calendars, this classification included only the very highest liturgical feasts. [C.H.]

2. From the chant at the lighting of the paschal candle during the Easter vigil: "*O happy fault*, which called for so great a Redeemer!" [C.H.]

SAINT JOHN

Review of *Christianity According to Saint John* by
W. F. Howard, and *The Christian Failure* by Charles
Singer; *Time and Tide*, 1943.

T he gospel of Saint John was for long a refuge for the
"spiritualizers" and a resort for the pseudo-mystics. It
seemed to contain little about baptism and little about
the eucharist, and nothing either way that could not
be interpreted out of a literal into an allegorical meaning. It could always be used as a blanket through which the
heavenly John cried to the not-nearly-so-heavenly Paul, busily
engaged on his work of complicating the simple spiritual gospel, "Hold! Hold!" Not that Paul did.

There was, of course, some excuse for this. It is true that
the fourth gospel is peculiarly the gospel of the Holy Spirit,
and that it particularly stresses the fact that all the events in
the life of our Lord, as well as happening in Judea, happen in
the soul; whereas the synoptics made it crashingly clear that
all events that happen in the soul happened in Judea. Why
this second fact should be thought a rather low business is always surprising. But so it was. That God should be born in
the spirit was permissible—not that he should be born in the
flesh; the new birth by inward fire—yes, the new birth by outward water—no; the mystical union—yes, the physical resurrection—no. And so on. All this the divine John was supposed, in

essence, to support—truth, but not dogma. (Though the picture of Truth tolerantly refusing to be dogmatic—!)

It becomes more and more clear that this division cannot be made. Saint John was as much one of the household of faith as Saint Matthew or Saint Paul; there is in him no escape from it into some little esoteric garden. The esotericism is there, but it is in the facts of earth as much as of heaven—say rather, it is in their being one. The church? "Jesus answered them, Did I not choose you the Twelve?" The eucharist? It is Saint John who describes the departure of those—no doubt, all of them mystics—who were shocked by its materialism. The priesthood? It is Saint John who records the commission—"whose soever sins ye remit, they are remitted; whose ye retain, they are retained." The awful subordination of heaven to earth, with every responsibility that it involves, is made more, not less, complex by the fourth gospel.

Dr. Howard's learned but never pedantic book is obviously the cause of this meditation. It is, one might say, a study in the words used, as all proper criticism must be. Dr. Howard has wonderfully avoided filling his pages with personal exhortations and semi-pious reverie. In consequence he remains fresh and interesting—especially perhaps in the chapter called "Eschatology and Mysticism." All Saint John's sublime mystical doctrine does not prevent his belief in a future *parousia*. The real distinction in all the gospels is identical; it is only, when the Voice (within or without; say, within and without, one Voice, one actual Voice) cries "Lo, I come quickly," between those who say simply "Come" and those who say "Come—but not *too* quickly."

It is convenient (for us who belong to the last group) to mention here Dr. Singer's little book on *The Christian Failure*. Dr. Singer is so passionately sincere, and his historical accusations are so justified by hideous facts, that it is not quite becoming to find fault with a book which all instructed

Christians would find it wholesome to read. But on his view the scientific discoveries of the Renaissance make nonsense of Saint John. When the universe was understood to be "infinite," it could no longer be supposed to be "created." "Creation is fundamental to Christianity." To Saint John indeed, as Dr. Howard shows, the characteristic of the whole universe, especially of man, is "creatureliness." If man is not a creature, Christianity is untrue. Dr. Singer expects a complete breakdown of the church. He believes that Christians have "minimized or slurred" the evils in the history of the church. I do not know that the Inquisition, Alexander VI, and Calvin (whom he gives as examples) have been much minimized. Finally, he accuses us of having betrayed the Jews to the Germans, in the sense that we did not, before the war, as Christians, denounce the persecution. It is a fervid, and perhaps just, rebuke.

Yet acknowledging Dr. Singer's accusations, it is still to be noted that a doctrinal abyss remains. The most fundamental Christian doctrine, Dr. Singer says, "anticipating even the Incarnation, is that there is a dignity and worth of the individual soul, for without that the Incarnation itself would be meaningless." It is very doubtful if this is the doctrine of Saint John. There it is the undignified and worthless who are to be redeemed; their only value is that they can be made something other. "The greatest concession to the dignity and worth of the individual is that he shall worship God as he believes God desires. That concession has never been made by Christianity." Nor by the prophets of Israel; see the terrible description of idolatry in Ezekiel. Freedom of adoration (within limits, I gather, that exclude the Thug) is a necessity. But the union of that necessity and the Christian necessity is one of the deepest and darkest of all unions. The light that shines in that darkness is not easily seen by easily-tolerant eyes.

AUGUSTINE AND ATHANASIUS

Review of F. J. Sheed's translation of the *Confessions*, and "A new translation by a Religious" of *The Incarnation of the Word of God* by Saint Athanasius; *Time and Tide*, 1944.

S aint Augustine has, on the whole, suffered more than Saint Athanasius from the sympathy of the "human-hearted" among his readers. The *Confessions* have become "one of the great autobiographies of the world." One might almost as well call the four gospels "the four best short biographies in the world." The *Confessions* are continually luring us to "fiddle harmonics on the strings of sensualism," or of sensibility, for it is not only carnality that is in question. Nowadays we read Shakespeare to discover that he suffered from insomnia; we read the *Cloud of Unknowing* to discover that its author was "a lovable man"; we remark with appreciative sympathy Augustine praying: "Give me chastity, but not yet." We are not, however, nearly so appreciative of the chastity which he undoubtedly got. Yet this is the dramatic climax of the story; to miss it is to miss Hamlet killing the king and only to be interested while the Prince wanders through the corridors of Elsinore. After the famous "Tolle: lege!"[1] our interest begins to flag. But for Augustine himself it was only then that the serious in-

terest began—when "our soul by living well begins to be a living soul."

No doubt the difficulty about chastity was one—only one—
of Augustine's personal difficulties. But the climax of the
book—the mere literary climax as a book—is only by accident
in the personal Augustine at all, even the chaste Augustine. It
was certainly not by accident that he made his own story end
with the tenth book of the *Confessions* and that the last three
books deal with the account of the creation of the world, in
Genesis. This was the full and great conclusion. Augustine
was issuing into a true and significant world of which Genesis
gave a mystical account. That is the whole point, and not to
feel it so is to be a bad literary critic. To disagree with him is
another matter, but not to see what he is doing is to betray
that very literature we claim to admire and safeguard.

Some of his interpretations will seem strange and strained,
as do some of the arguments of Athanasius; just as some of
Shakespeare's jokes seem dull, and some of Milton's lines
flat. But what both these writers were talking about is quite
clear: it was "a new heaven and a new earth," not in the future but all about them. Our Lord had promised them this
world back "a hundred fold," as well as eternal life, and to
their own intense and joyous surprise they found they had
got it. They were in this new genesis—*tam antiqua, tam
nova*[2]—and they wrote about it. It renewed their intelligence
as well as their virtue. The *Confessions* devote more space to
philosophy than to chastity, and the sense of enlargement is
very marked. Speaking of that anthropomorphism of which
Christians were, then as now, accused, Augustine, when he
discovered what they really believed, burst out: "I rejoiced, O
my God, that Your church...had no taste for such puerile
nonsense." A sentence less quoted than the famous "but not
yet" passage is that in which he mocks at himself for having
"gone on spouting forth so many uncertainties as confidently

as if I had known them for sure." But then the admission of a fornication or two is much more to our taste than the acknowledgement that we solemnly talked twaddle for years. The humility which Augustine found—say rather, that blossoming humility which in that new world *was* Augustine—enabled him to make both admissions in passing. This was what living in "the reasonable and intellectual mind of Your pure City" permitted.

The treatise of Saint Athanasius is one of the Christian classics. It is much to be desired that we may have more of such books, if they can be as clearly done. Athanasius begins with the same fact with which Augustine ends: "The first fact that you must grasp is this: the renewal of creation has been wrought by the Self-same Word Who made it in the beginning." He is, of course, arguing and not telling a story, but he is arguing about the same subject—this renewal of the corrupt into in corruption. "All things," says Fox, "gave up a new smell unto me." "Herein," wrote Law, "appears the high dignity and never-ceasing perpetuity of our nature." It is not merely a personal salvation, though naturally this great and universal thing can only be known through personal salvation; you can only live in England by being in England and only in "the pure City" by being in the pure City. That is what salvation is. The knowledge of it is close enough—entirely human and utterly different, unbearably intimate and unbearably distant. "All this fantasy," says Athanasius, of oracles and magic and inspirations, "has ceased," and it is that phrase which permeates all these great writers. They say, as it were, "I do not mean to sound arrogant; I do not want to seem rude; it is not I who say so; but all this fantasy of yours has ceased. Incorruption exists; this is it. Smell, look, taste, handle: this is creation made new." "I heard," wrote Augustine, "I understood."

Endnotes

1. At the crucial moment in his conversion, Augustine heard a child chanting *"Tolle: lege—*take: read." He opened at random to Rom. 13:13 and his uncertainty vanished; *Confessions* VIII 12. [C.H.]

2. "Late have I loved you, O Beauty *so ancient, so new"*; *Confessions* X 27. [C.H.]

THE THEOLOGY of
ROMANTIC LOVE

Dorothy Sayers found in all Williams's literary criticism, and especially his interpretations of Dante, a "power of evoking a very present and demanding life from that which might be supposed decently dead and sterilized." This chapter from *He Came Down from Heaven* (from which the first paragraph has been omitted) is perhaps the best introduction not only to Williams's reading of Dante but also to his own "romantic theology."

I n the centuries after the passing of Christ there grew up in Europe a great metaphysical civilization, a society as much based on a philosphical principle as the first Roman Empire had been on the evasion of philosophical principles. The fundamental idea was salvation. The grand substitution had been, and was being, carried out, and society was to be organized on the basis of a belief in substitution and salvation. It had, of course, many other elements; it had something of the Precursor, and a very great deal of Pharaoh, but it thought in terms of the apostles. The celebration of the Mass did not so much prolong the sacrifice in time as turn time back to the sacrifice; communion mystically

united the pious to heaven and the impious to hell; the ceremony of penance was instituted to spread everywhere the
public news of a secret pardon. To the naturally outstanding
figures of kings, conquerors, law-givers, and even poets, were
now added the supernaturally outstanding figures of those
who, by a passion of courtesy towards God and man, seemed
even on earth to have fully lost their own lives and attained
some other.

Experience underwent new interpretation. The revolution,
which had been assumed by Christ as a preliminary to the
kingdom, became entangled with the principles of the church,
and has (to the irritation of both groups of minds) remained
somewhat entangled. The revolution may exist without any
demand for the church, but the church has never existed long
anywhere without creating a demand for a revolution. "The
poor ye have always with you," said Christ, and wherever his
tradition has gone we have been made acutely aware of them.
The idea of social justice became important. The idea of tragedy lost its importance—almost its nature. In this world all
was, in the end, under Providence, however detestable the
enemies of Providence; as when, in one of his loveliest passages, Dante speaks of Luck as being one of the primal creatures, who forever enjoys her own beatitude, while fools
blaspheme her below. Nor could the other world be tragic,
since there could hardly be tragedy, whatever grief, in a
man's obstinate determination to be damned. So death at
once gained and lost; it gained in frightfulness and in beauty;
it lost the profound solace of Lucretius, for immortality
(whether a boon or a curse) was now a fact, and final oblivion
was forbidden to comfort man's mind. All these alterations
filled men's pre-eminent moments with new nourishment and
new repair. The imagination of the world and of heaven had
changed.

Of all these alterations one affected perhaps more than all the rest (except for the central dogmas) the casual fancies and ordinary outlook of men and women. As a historic fact the change has been described, in words better than any I could find, by C.S. Lewis, in one of the most important critical books of our time, *The Allegory of Love*. I may therefore quote him at some length:

> It seems to us natural that love should be the commonest theme of serious imaginative literature: but a glance at classical antiquity or at the Dark Ages at once shows us that what we took for 'nature' is really a special state of affairs, which will probably have an end, and which certainly had a beginning in eleventh-century Provence. It seems—or it seemed to us till lately—a natural thing that love (under certain conditions) should be regarded as a noble and ennobling passion: it is only if we imagine ourselves trying to explain this doctrine to Aristotle, Virgil, Saint Paul, or the author of *Beowulf,* that we become aware how far from natural it is....
>
> French poets, in the eleventh century, discovered or invented, or were the first to express, that romantic species of passion which English poets were still writing about in the nineteenth. They effected a change which has left no corner of our ethics, our imagination, or our daily life untouched, and they erected impassable barriers between us and the classical past or the Oriental present. Compared with this revolution the Renaissance is a mere ripple on the surface of literature....
>
> The new thing itself I do not pretend to explain. Real changes in human sentiment are very rare—there are perhaps three or four on record—but I believe that they occur, and that this is one of them.

There entered into the relations between the sexes a philosophical, even a religious, idea.[1] That idea had a very long life before it, and was to undergo many unfortunate and fortunate chances. On the one hand, like many other religious ideas, it was to become a superstition; on the other hand, it was to be, naturally but regrettably, cold-shouldered by the ecclesiastical authorities. It was to be an indulgence to the populace and a stumbling-block to the puritans—using both words of intellectual states of mind. It was to save and endanger souls. And it is still quite uncertain what will happen to it. It may utterly disappear from the earth. But if not, the popular idea of it will probably have to undergo a good deal of purification. In fact, and in itself, it is a thing not of superstition and indulgence, but of doctrine and duty, and not of achievement but of promise.

The pre-eminent moment of romantic love is not, of course, confined to the moment of romantic sex love. There are other moments of intense experience combined with potentiality of further experience. Great art has it and politics and nature and (it is said) maturity. But few of these have had the same universality and few, owing to the chance of genius, have undergone the same analysis. Wordsworth began the task of the analysis of man's experience of nature as a precursor and means to something greater, but for various reasons he left it unfinished. Nature, until recently, had become as much of a superstition as romantic love; it looks, however, as if it would have a shorter period of influence.

The difficulty in any discussion of such experiences is in the finding common ground for discussion. There is no accepted agreement upon what the state which our grandfathers used to call "falling in love" involves. It is neither sex appetite pure and simple; nor, on the other hand, is it necessarily related to marriage. It is something like a state of adoration, and it has been expressed, of course, by the poets better than by anyone else. Perhaps, therefore, the most convenient way of defining it will be to take a quotation from one of them, and that not from any of the more extreme romantics but from Milton (who has long enough been regarded as both pious and puritanical). It has here the additional advantage of being imagined as spoken by Adam of Eve, and therefore as an imagined expression of that state of the good in which, before the Fall, they existed. It comes from *Paradise Lost*, Book 8, 546-59:

> *...when I approach*
> *her loveliness, so absolute she seems*
> *And in herself complete, so well to know*
> *Her own, that what she wills to do or say*
> *Seems wisest, virtuousest, discreetest, best.*
> *All higher knowledge in her presence falls*
> *Degraded: Wisdom in discourse with her*
> *Loses, discount'nanced, and like Folly shows:*
> *Authority and Reason on her wait,*
> *As one intended first, not after made*
> *Occasionally; and, to consummate all,*
> *Greatness of mind and nobleness their seat*
> *Build in her loveliest, and create an awe*
> *About her, as a guard angelic placed.*

This then is the contemplation of the object of love from a state of romantic love. There has been and is, now as always, only one question about this state of things: is it serious? is it capable of intellectual treatment? is it capable of belief, labor, fruition? is it (in some sense or other) *true?* It is, of course, true to Adam if the vision has so appeared to him. It was certainly a vision, to Adam, and in the poem, of something like the kingdom of heaven on earth; Eve is at once an inhabitant of the kingdom and the means by which the kingdom is seen. Can this state of things be treated as the first matter of a great experiment? and if so, what exactly is the material? and what exactly are the best conditions of the experiment? The end, of course, is known by definition of the kingdom: it is the establishment of a state of *caritas*, of pure love, the mode of expansion of one moment into eternity. It is, in fact, another example of the operation of the inclusive-exclusive thing; only in this case it is Adam, in the poem, and we, outside the poem, who are expected to do something about it.

There was, in the history of Christendom, a genius of the greatest power whose imagination worked on this theme, and that was Dante. The range of his whole work provides a complete account of the making of the experiment and of its success. It is not, of course, the only theme in Dante: *tot homini quot Dantes.*[2] But at least it is one, and it happens to be one which he very consciously asserted. We shall not therefore be ingeniously extracting a gospel from him of which he knew nothing if we believe him. (There used certainly to be some critics who maintained that there never was a girl in Dante's life at all; at least, any denial of Beatrice must mean this or it means nothing. Once let any girl in—including Gemma Donati—and the principle has been admitted, and only the details can be discussed.) It is not possible here to make any effort to trace the whole philosophical journey. All that can be done is to take, because it is done so much better than we can do it, an analysis here and there.

The journey begins in the *New Life* with the first meeting with Beatrice at the age of nine, and with the second meeting at the age of eighteen. It proceeds through every kind of concern until it ends, at almost the close of the *Comedy*, with a state in which those first Beatrician encounters, which were once full of such a thrilling *tremendum*, seem almost paltry, except that they were the beginning of all, compared to the massive whole of single and exchanged Love. In reaching the end, we reach (as in all poetry) the beginning also; the *New*

Life, like the *Hell* and the *Purgatory*, exists only by, in, and for the *Paradise* that includes them.

The description of the Beatrician encounters is in the *New Life*. A more intellectual and analytical definition is in the *Banquet*. It is true that it there occurs because of another lady, the "Lady of the Window," but that does not alter the definitions. The great love poets may have been monogamic in the sense of having one lady at a time; it cannot be said that they had one lady all the time. Nor indeed can it very easily be maintained that Dante was a striking example of New Testament monogamy, considering the extent to which his imagination concentrated itself on one woman while he was married to another. It is part of the incredible irony of the kingdom of heaven that it should produce the most stupendous and scientific statement of the experiment from a poet whom the stricter moralists of the experiment are compelled to disavow or to disguise.

The experience of romantic love then is described in the *New Life* and analyzed in the *Banquet*. The intellect is always called on to do its part. The appearance of Beatrice and her image is of so noble a virtue that "at no time it suffered Love to rule over me without the faithful council of Reason in things where such council was useful." The first appearance of Beatrice produces three separate effects: it moves the heart as the seat of spiritual emotions, the brain as the center of perception, and the liver as the place of corporal emotions. It is much to be wished that English literature had kept liver as well as heart; we have to use one word for both emotional states—what (reverting to the old ambiguity of heaven) we might call the spiritual and the spatial heaven of romantic love. Dante did his part in describing the spatial heavens, but it is the spiritual which are here the concern. The following points may be briefly noted.[3]

(1) The intellect "in discoursing of her, many times wished to infer things about her, though I could not understand them." The experience—the sight, that is, of the beloved—arouses a sense of intense significance, a sense that an explanation of the whole universe is being offered, and indeed in some sense understood; only it cannot yet be defined. Even when the intellect seems to apprehend, it cannot express its purpose; "the tongue cannot follow that which the intellect sees."

(2) "She is...the pattern of man's essence existing in thought within the divine mind...she is as completely perfect as the essence of man can possibly be." She is, that is, the perfect center and norm of humanity; others exist, it seems, because and in so far as, they resemble her virtue. The extraordinary vision is that of the ordinary thing *in excelsis*.

(3) "The experiences which may be had of her in these operations which are peculiar to the rational soul, into which the divine light radiates with less hindrance, I mean in speech and in the acts which may be called behaviour and carriage." It is a convention of love-poetry to speak of light emanating from the person of the beloved; the dichotomy of metaphysics is between those who believe that it does and those who do not. This does not seem to be arguable. The forehead and the hand are radiant; she disseminates glory. Or they do not, and she does not; if it seems so, it does but seem. But no lover was ever content to allow that it was but a seeming; rather, it is to be that portion of the divine light which, in the eternal creation of her in heaven, possesses her. "The light that lightens every man that comes into the world" is made visible through her, by the will of grace, and by that alone. It seems that no one yet discovered that light of glory in any woman or any man by hunting for it; it seems that it may exist where it is not wanted. It has its own methods; "My ways are not your ways, saith the Lord." It is not of a nature certainly to ri-

val the electric light, but whether that is due to its weakness or to the lover's imperfection is another matter. The schools are divided.

(4) "This lady is a thing visibly miraculous, of which the eyes of men may daily have experience, and this marvel makes all others possible in our eyes...this lady with her wondrous aspect assists our faith. Therefore was she from eternity so ordained." By "faith" there Dante means faith in "him who was crucified"—but then to Dante he who was crucified was a thing natural and fundamental, and not odd and all religious. It is perhaps rather the word "eternity" which is here suggestive. She appears with this quality, as of something unaffected by time; it is the metaphysical association of the visible light. She is the substance of spirit.

(5) "I affirm, therefore, that, since we have now ascertained the meaning of this section in which this lady is extolled with regard to her soul, one must now go on to perceive how...I extol her with regard to her body. And I say that in her aspect things appear which reveal some of the joys (among the many other joys) of Paradise. The noblest pleasure...is to feel content, and this is the same as to be blest; and this pleasure, although in a different way, is truly found in the aspect of this lady...with much pleasure does her beauty feed the eyes of those who behold her. But this contentment is different in kind from that felt in Paradise, which is everlasting; for this everlasting contentment cannot fall to anyone here." The two places where the beauty of the soul most chiefly appears are the eyes and the mouth, and it is the integrity and modesty of the lady that are there mostly to be admired; one may say, the right proportion of candor and restraint, the perfect balance of virtue, opposed yet coexistent.

(6) Her beauty "surpasses our intellect as the sun surpasses weak sight, not indeed that which is healthy and strong." The weak sight of the mind cannot properly contem-

plate this beauty, for "after gazing freely on it, the soul becomes intoxicated, so that she goes astray in all her operations." This saying is reminiscent of Messias: "blessed is he whosoever shall not be offended at me," to whom I am not a cause of greater evil. The glory is apt to dazzle the beholder unless he already has a mind disposed to examine the pattern of the glory. It is more important to do the work of the kingdom than to say "Lord, Lord." Indeed, it is by some such going astray that the theology of romantic love has been neglected in favor of the superstitions and fables. The effort after the pattern marks the difference. The superstitions make heaven and earth in the form of the beloved; the theology declares that the beloved is the first preparatory form of heaven and earth. Its controlling maxim is that these things are first seen through Beatrice as a means; the corollary is that they are found through Beatrice as a first means only. The preposition refers not only to sight but to progress. For

(7) "Her beauty has power to renovate nature in those who behold her, which is a marvellous thing. And this confirms what has been said...that she is the helper of our faith." This is perhaps the most profound, most universal, and most widely confirmed saying of all. It is the Dantean equivalent of all the resolutions and reformations rashly attributed to the influence of the beloved. It is also the Dantean equivalent of the first coming of the kingdom. He says, soon after: "She was created not only to make a good thing better, but also to turn a bad thing into good." Things intolerable outside a state of love become blessed within: laughter and love convert for a moment the dark habitations within the soul to renewed gardens in Eden. The primal knowledge is restored, and something like pardon restores something like innocence. The "new life" exists. It cannot continue to exist permanently without faith and labor. Nothing that comes down from heaven can. But it renews nature if only for a moment;

it flashes for a moment into the lover the life he was meant to possess instead of his own by the exposition in her of the life she was meant to possess instead of her own. They are "in love."

(8) "This is she who maketh humble all the self-willed; she was the thought of him who set the universe in motion." She is the phenomenon of the center; and the chief grace she bestows is humility—the self-forgetfulness which (only) makes room for adoration. She is the vision of the divine glory and the means of the divine grace, and she herself is irresponsible for it and almost irrelevant to it. She is the Mother of Love—of *caritas*, and even of a *caritas* beyond any *caritas* we can imagine; she is the chosen Mother of the goodwill of God.

These then are certain of the definitions which Dante gives of the effect of the appearance of Beatrice. It must be left to any reader to decide how far they form—at least partially—a correct account of a young man in the state of having "fallen in love." *Mutatis mutandis*, they may apply to the woman; though, since she is not in Dante, it is rather to Milton's Eve that we must go for a description of her. It is a not unpleasant thought that the word Fall occurs in this experience also; as if the divine grace, after man had insisted on falling once into a divided and contradictory knowledge, had arranged itself to trick him into an unexpected fall into restored and single knowledge. The inclusive-exclusive is a marked sign here of the means of salvation. Eve, Beatrice, or whoever, is certainly her peculiar and (in vision) indefectible self. But she is also the ordinary girl exalted into this extraordinary; she is the norm of all ladies, even if the others do not seem (in the lover's vision) to reach it. The union of flesh and spirit, visible in her (or him), is credible everywhere; indeed, that union, which so much poetry has desired to describe, is understood as more profound and more natural than the dichotomy, of experience or of expression, which has separated them. She is inclusive of both, and exclusive of their separateness. She is, in a final paradox, inclusive even of moments when she is none of these things, and the grace of that state is not least revealed when it excludes itself, as it were, and includes a happy and temporary ignorance of glory in favor of contented play.

The *New Life* had already personified the definitions of the *Banquet*. In the earlier book Beatrice is presented as having on Dante the effect which the *Banquet* analyzes. She exists (actual or not, but preferably, on the mere evidence, actual) as a form incarnating what is only afterwards understood as "the idea or abstraction of its kind." She meets him, and he her, in the activities of the city; ordinary things happen, and two extraordinary—for she snubs him, and she dies. Two or three incidents bear on the idea of her relation to God. The first is the moment when the girl comes down the street and says "Good morning" in passing. This thrilling and universal moment is known as "the salutation of Beatrice." So, of course, it is, and it is as serious (but not as artistic) as that. It is the flash of the moment in a word. Dante says: "I say that when she appeared from any place, there was through my hope of her admirable salutation, no enemy remaining to me, but a flame of *caritas* possessed me, which made me pardon anyone who had offended me; and if anyone had then asked me concerning anything, my answer would have been only *Love*, with a face clothed in humility." Or more colloquially: "I say that when she came along, I was so thrilled with the mere hope that she would notice me that I was friends with everyone, and utterly full of goodwill, and I was ready to forgive anyone who had offended me. If I had been asked any question at all I should have answered quite humbly *Love*." The pardon is not a cold superior thing but inevitably produced by *una fiamma di caritade*, a leaping momentary fire of pure love, like the fiery heavenly creatures of Ezekiel. It is accompanied by a communication of humility, as from the source, i.e. that kingdom of heaven which declared in a paradox of divine vitality: "I am meek and lowly of heart." Dante does not suggest that he has already achieved a state of humility and pure love; the whole point is that they are unusually summoned up in him by the girl's greeting. To discover the method by which they become habitual and essential is the aim of the grand experiment, and was at least one of the themes of his imagination; to find the point of change of stress, and therefore of significance, so that at the end of the *Comedy* Beatrice properly turns her eyes away from him.

> *Così orai; ed ella sì lontana,*
> *come parea, sorrise e riguar dommi;*
> *poi si tornò all'eterna fontana.*

> Thus I prayed; seeming so far,
> she smiled and she gazed back,
> then turned to the eternal spring.

Dante does similarly; he begins to lose consciousness even of her as the full immingled zones of beatitude open; the early refusal of the salutation which had been "the loss of my beatitude" and an agony is now the very pulse of the final exaltation. In what sense, if ever, Beatrice looks at him again is a thing for consideration only in a more detailed study of the Comedy, from the other end of the *Paradise*.

The second incident is more allegorical, but the allegory is almost a symbolism; that is, it has almost not a likeness but an identity. Dante one day sees another young woman coming along. The whole of the *New Life* is full of other young women, but, whatever they may have been in his life, they are in his imagination part of the inclusiveness of the exclusive thing; they are very necessary and quite unimportant—what one might call a general sex-awareness without credibility. This one is the lover of one of his friends; her name is Giovanna or Joan; she is so lovely that she has been nicknamed Primavera or Spring. Beatrice was coming at a little distance behind. Love then said to Dante: "If you consider her first name, it is as much as to say Primavera, for her name Giovanna is from that Giovanni which preceded the true light, saying: 'I am the voice of one crying in the wilderness, Prepare the way of the Lord'....He who is willing to consider with subtlety would call Beatrice Love, for the great similarity she has to me." It would be perhaps unsafe to do so; if by Love is meant the passion of goodwill and humility. But it would be safe to call her the Mother of Love in the soul. The comparison of Giovanna with the Precursor, with that John who preceded *"la verace luce,"* makes her the precursor of the divine light which in Beatrice radiates, as was said in the *Banquet,* "with less hindrance." The Divine Thing of goodwill and humility which Dante had experienced springs from his experience of Beatrice; she is the Mother of the grace, and even therefore of the occult God. It is a result of the Incarnation that opened all potentialities of the knowledge of the kingdom of heaven in and through matter. "My covenant shall be in your flesh."

The third point can only be mentioned; it is the death of Beatrice. No doubt, of Beatrice, assuming Beatrice; the fact need not be denied because it means a great deal more than itself. For nothing seems to be more certain than that the original glory, the *Beatricianness* of Beatrice, does either disappear or at least modify itself. In this also we have an exclusive-inclusive event. Beatrice dies; that is the exclusive. The light and beatitude disappear; that is the inclusive. In the imagination the two need not be hostile, nor in fact. "The City is widowed," says Dante, quoting Jeremiah. It is apt to be a blow.

When she returns she comes as a judgment. But also her own nature is more particularly declared. It is declared in a very different kind of poem. But what is declared there is in accord with all that had gone before. The first encounter with Beatrice had awakened physical, mental, and spiritual awareness; later encounters had communicated to Dante moments of humility and pure love, however far he might be from staying in them; she had followed Giovanna as Christ followed John. And she dies, and things happen, and this and the other interferes, and Dante in imagination comes to himself in a savage wood, at the foot of a great hill. The hill is "the cause and occasion of all joy." He tries to climb; he is driven back by the whole of human life understood in its three great images of the gay and beautiful Leopard of youth, the strong and haughty Lion of middle age, and the terrible insatiable Wolf of old age. These which make up Time, or make up at least all of Time that matters to Dante, drive him back from that mountain which seems to arise beyond Time into a place which seems also to lie beyond Time, the place "*dove il sol tace*," where the sun is silent, where even Virgil seems but a faint ghost. Virgil is—Virgil, but he is (because of that) poetry, wisdom, institutions, the things that in fact he had been in the world when the great organization of the empire was formed: all—except the Incarnation.

Dante imagines himself here as not able to move on the direct way, as he had in an earlier book imagined Beatrice as dying. He has to go round, through the knowledge of sin and the hellish people "who have lost the good of intellect." He has to find another way to the mountain, but when he comes to the ascent he still approaches it under the light of Venus, the dawn star, "the fair planet which hearkens to love." He has to go through the purging of all sins—especially (he says) of pride. He has to listen to the great discourse of Virgil on the nature of love and the terrible malignancy of the sin which is envy and jealousy and pride. He comes, at the top of the mountain, to the earthly paradise of Eden; he sees the procession breaking out of the air, the procession which is the "pageant of the church." But the final figure of the pageant of the church is Beatrice—it is, in fact, a pageant of Beatrice. He sees her; he feels *"d'antico amor...la gran potenza"*; he feels the hot embers *"dell' antica fiamma,"* and he is answered with what has been called almost the greatest line in Dante and therefore in all poetry:

> *Guardaci ben: ben sem, ben sem, Beatrice.*
>
> Look well: we are, indeed we are, Beatrice.

It is afterwards that he paradisally recovers the perfect knowledge of the good, by drinking of Lethe which removes the knowledge of evil as evil, by drinking of Eunoe which communicates the knowledge of good (even evil) as good. Between the two he sees Beatrice facing the two-natured gryphon of Christ, and he sees in her eyes the reflection of those two natures. Those eyes are not different; they are the very eyes "from which Love began to shoot his arrows at you." Here, surrounded by angels, prophets, evangelists, virtues, romantic love is seen to mirror the humanity and deity of the Redeemer. He sees it; "my soul tasted the food which makes hungry where most it satisfies"—so to combine two poets. It is then that he enters the first heaven where Piccarda, asked if she does not envy those in greater heavens their more glorious fate, answers: "Brother, our will is quiet in the strength of love...here love is fate." All the exchanges of heaven lie open.

But really, though he now imagined it more clearly and more strongly, he had not known anything different, in essence or in principle, when the face of the Florentine girl flashed her "Good morning" at him along the street of their city.

The chance of a phrase joins the theology of romantic love to the theology of the church. In the *New Life*, at one point,

Beatrice snubs Dante; she "denies him her salutation." She had, he says, heard "outrageous rumors" about him. After this Love appeared to him in a vision, and said, *"Ego tamquam centrum circuli cui simili modo se habent circumferentiae partes, tu autem non sic."*[4] Love refused to explain this, but without presuming to do what Love would not do, one may at least remark that Dante had experienced humility and good will through the salutation. When the salutation was refused, he was plunged into anything but humility and good will; his beatitude was denied. But Love itself is not so subjected to outward wants. I do not press that Love should here be taken as allegorically equal to Christ; I am inclined to think that this develops in the *New Life* but is certainly not there at the beginning. But Love is certainly sufficiently full of *caritas* to know that he himself is in the center and unaffected by such things on the circumference of experience as salutations and responses; only with Dante it is not so, or not yet.

About the same time Bonaventure was writing that God was a circle whose center was everywhere and its circumference nowhere. The diagram of process is clear. Dante is on the circumference, and the things that happen there make a difference to him; he has with them no fixed and always equal relation: only he sees the center. The Love of the *New Life* is in the center; to it all parts of the circumference, all times, all experiences, have this equal relation. In humility and good will Dante answered Love when things went well, but Love answers Love however things go. But beyond that is the state when there is, in effect, no circumference; or rather, every point of the circumference is at the center, for the circumference itself is *caritas*, and relation is only between the center and the center. This is love-in-heaven.

I have said that I have taken these things—so few of so many—from Dante because they are the expressions of the greatest European poet (greatest as poet, not only as meta-physician) and because no one else has given us so complete an exposition of the Way of Romantic Love. It is, of course, on his own terms; the Way can be followed though the terms are rejected. But at least the Way understood in other terms must not be less than his. It is possible to follow this method of love without introducing the name of God. But it is hardly possible to follow it without proposing and involving as an end a state of *caritas* of the utmost possible height and breadth, nor without allowing to matter a significance and power which (of all the religions and philosophies) only Christianity has affirmed.

If, however, we retain the name and idea of God, and if there is any common agreement about the state of exalted experience known as the state of "falling in love," then it is possible to go further and relate that experience to the Incarnation of the kingdom. When Messias said: "Behold my mother" he was, in this relation, merely accurate. The beloved (male or female) is seen in the light of a paradisal knowledge and experience of good. Christ exists in the soul, in joy, in terror, in a miracle of newness. *Ecce, omnia nova facio.*[5] He who is the mystical child of the lovers sustains and supports them: they are the children of their child. "We speak that we do know and testify that we have seen. ...No man hath ascended up into heaven, but he that came down from heaven, even the Son of Man which is in heaven."

A theology of this kind will be at the disadvantage of all other kinds of theology, and give rise (within itself) to heresies. Extremists of one kind will claim for the beloved a purity as nonexistent as the purity of the church militant upon earth. Her, or his, humanity is an extremely maculate humanity, and all the worship under heaven ought not to prevent her lover from knowing (with reasonable accuracy and unreasonable love) when she is lazy, lewd, or malicious. She has a double nature, and he can have double sight. On the other hand it will be supposed that the death of Beatrice implies the nonexistence of Beatrice; that the disappearance of the glory implies the falsity of the glory. A similar disappearance has not been supposed to invalidate the fact and authority of Christ, and the quiet piety—often the extremely quiet piety—of Christians has (justly) been permitted to relate itself to the glory of the Transfiguration. The "quiet affection" of so many prophecies by the aged might be allowed a similar relation. Quiet piety and quiet affection have their place in the kingdom, but we need not force on them an imperialism they never ought to have at the expense of other more vivid forms of glory and of grace. Nor can the denial or disparagement of those who have forgotten or not experienced it diminish its authority.

It is perhaps a pity that the clergy as a whole are so often among the disparagers. A natural hesitation over the uncovenanted graces leads them not so much to say wrong things as to say the right things in the wrong tone. Their proper concern with one rule of morality leads them to be careless of another. The Divine Thing that made itself the foundation of the church does not seem, to judge by his comments on the religious leaders of his day, ever to have hoped much from officers of a church. The most he would do was to promise that the gates of hell should not *prevail* against it. It is about all that, looking back on the history of the church, one can feel they have not done.

Hell has made three principal attacks on the Way of Romantic Love. The dangerous assumptions produced are: (1) the assumption that it will naturally be everlasting; (2) the assumption that it is personal; (3) the assumption that it is sufficient. Similar dangers have attacked other ways in the kingdom; the instance will he remembered of the London churchwarden who had always supposed himself to be a true

Christian until one day he realized, in a flash of clarity, that Christ was dogmatically asserted to have died for all men—especially some few whom he strongly disliked and others whom he extremely despised. He therefore, with great good sense, abandoned his profession of Christianity in favor of a free hand with his emotions.

(1) The assumption that the Beatrician state is everlasting is false. "The right faith is that we believe and confess" that it is eternal but is not everlastingly visible, any more than the earthly life of Christ. Its quality may deceive hasty imagination, and it may be expected to return quickly as was Christ by the church. It may not. Its authority remains unimpaired. The emotional vows, however, springing from its original state, do not at all times appear so possible or desirable. On the other hand, it seems to be true that there is at first a very strong desire in the two lovers to maintain and conduct forever this experiment towards *caritas* between themselves, and certainly some kind of pledged fidelity would seem to be a condition of the experiment. The church has maintained that (under certain conditions) exchanged vows of this kind should be regarded as final. It has even maintained (justly) that, as in certain cases, the state of love leads to marriage, so marriage can lead to a more advanced state of love, and since, on the whole hypothesis, this is the only desirable thing, it may be right in its discipline. (The natural tendency to falsify evidence in favor of a point of view does not perhaps prevail more strongly here than elsewhere.) But the matter of marriage is a subject different from the present and of too lofty a nature to be contented with a paragraph. The appearance of the glory is temporary; the authority of the glory towards pure love is everlasting; the quality of the glory is eternal, such as the heavens have in Christ.

(2) The second assumption is that the state of love is a personal possession; that is, (i) that it is the personal adornment

of the beloved; (ii) that it belongs personally to the lover. This mistake is hardly possible in the first state of humility. But the fallen state of man produces—again as in religion—something remarkably like a tendency to regard the revelation and the glory as one's own private property. Once the emotions have yielded to that falsity, the intellect too often is either thwarted or even betrayed into supporting them. Until a state of sanctity has been achieved, there will no doubt always be something proud or possessive in our attitude towards the thing that is called love. But, on the whole hypothesis, love does not belong to lovers, but they to it. It is their job, as it is their direction, and salvation.

It is for this reason that all such sins as envy and jealousy are mortal. Jealousy does not mean only sex-jealousy; it need not even relate to the lovers at all. Once the authority of the glory has been admitted, all jealousy and envy are against the idea of and the way to *caritas*, but the "all" must include the sexual. One can hardly keep jealousy out of the office but let it in to the home. It is, always and everywhere, idolatry; it is a desire to retain the glory for oneself, which means that one is not adoring the glory but only one's own relation to the glory. It ought perhaps, for fear of misunderstanding, to be added that the strictest monogamist ought to disapprove of jealousy as strongly as anyone else; the two things are entirely separate. But it must be admitted that we might be a little nearer, intellectually, to pure love if jealousy had been as passionately denounced as divorce in the Christian church. The envious man identifies the kingdom with himself, and by a frantic effort to retain the outward manifestation of the kingdom destroys it in himself, and with it his capacity to see it outside himself. A sin which is, by its essence, destructive of good will is worse than a sin which need not be, in its essence, more than disordered good will. Virgil proclaimed the difference; the one kind are bewailed in the place where they dwell who have lost the good of intellect, the other in the secular terraces of the Mountain of Purgatory. There is but one permissible state to any who have seen love: *"una fiamma di caritade,"* "a flame of love."

(3) The third assumption is even easier than the others: that it is sufficient to have known that state of love. A kind of Calvinism seizes the emotions; the heart has recognized the attributed perfection and stops there. It feels as if of the elect, and it goes on feeling that till it ceases to feel anything. It may recognize a social duty to be useful to others, to feed the poor. "Though I give all my goods...and have not charity it profiteth me nothing." To be in love must be followed by the will to *be* love; to be love to the beloved, to be love to all, to be in fact (as the Divine Thing said) perfect.

The alternative is to become the Sir Willoughby Patternes[6] of the spiritual life, and more unbearable even than Meredith's original. Shakespeare gave us the healthy opposite and limit in that as in so much (he, the everlasting corrector of the follies of the disciples of Dante); in our consciousness of such things as regards ourselves we had better not go further than the point at which "with a pure blush we may come off withal."

But, independent of any personal error, the vision has remained. It is not limited to love between the sexes, nor to any love. The use of the word (so spoilt has it become) in some sense colors it with the horrid tint of a false adoration and a pseudo-piety. But grace remains grace whatever fruits are grown from it. The experience of communicated humility and goodwill is the experience of the grace of reality and of the kingdom. The kingdom came down from heaven and was incarnate; since then and perhaps (because of it) before then, it is beheld through and in a carnality of joy. The beloved—person or thing—becomes the Mother of Love; Love is born in the soul; it may have its passion there; it may have its resurrection. It has its own divine nature united with our undivine nature. In such a doctrine the gospels take on other meanings. The light that lighteth every man is seen without as well as within. But that, by definition, is the nature of the kingdom.

Endnotes

1. I am aware that in the Middle Ages this idea involved conventionally certain conditions, but since they are not of its intellectual essence they need not be here considered.

2. "There are as many Dantes as there are men." [C.H.]

3. They are taken from sections 3-8 of the third treatise of the *Convivio*; the translation is from W.W. Jackson's version published by the Clarendon Press.

4. "I am like the center of a circle, to which the parts of the circumference are related in the same way, but with you it is not so." [C.H.]

5. "Behold, I make all things new." [C.H.]

6. Sir Willoughby Patterne is the chief character in George Meredith's novel *The Egotist* (1879), a singularly joyless man. [C.H.]

THE RENEWAL of CONTRITION

The Descent of the Dove, Williams's history of the church—or, as he put it, of the Holy Spirit in the church—follows for the most part the conventional divisions of European history. This is the Renaissance-and-Reformation chapter. Unconventional in most other respects, it gives a representative sample of Williams's gifts, if not as an original scholar, certainly as an interpreter of history. Especially noteworthy are the way he draws the contrast between the Renaissance and the Middle Ages, and his discussion of the debate over the relative importance of faith and works.

I n that new and grand outbreak of wealth and diverted energy [which was the Renascence], it can be seen that the effort to impose upon the half-converted masses the great complex of exchange rooted in redemption had failed. The effort had been made by means of the continual effort towards conversion, through generation after generation, and by the imposition of authoritative command. From the pope to the acolyte, from the king to the serf, from the scholastic doctor to the least actor in the Mysteries, the effort of converting disobedience through obedience to a love of reconciliation in obedience had failed, and the effort of compelling obedience by the force of the mere organized means of reconciliation had failed. It was not, of course, surprising; it was what had always been foreseen. Christendom had betrayed itself again, as, since Saint Peter, it was always doing. There was to be, as there always has been, a sharp and violent recall. It was not for nothing that Messias had uttered one of his most appalling and ambiguous sayings: "Behold, I am with you always."

The particular state of things which we call medieval drew to its end in an outbreak of energy, and sometimes a rather feverish energy. The Middle Ages did not know that they were ending but they did know that they were changing. They knew that the East had fallen and that the Turk, that Islam and its Unincarnate Deity, were in Constantinople, and threatening the West. They knew also that antiquity had returned— in manuscripts, in statues, in prestige. They knew that navigation was expanding. They knew, in fact, that their own Victorian age was past and that a whole new mode of living was at their disposal; they were the heirs of everything. Over all Europe went up a kind of scream of color. The Middle Ages had had both screams and color; they had had enough worldliness. But formally they had always, at a certain point, intended to dissociate themselves from worldliness. The admiration there paid to the glory of man, of *homo*, had been checked by an awareness of the need of the New Birth. The Renascence tended to forget the need for any other birth but its own.

The traditional figure of the Renascence used to be Alexander VI. It is impossible not a little to regret the rehabilitation of the Borgias. To remember that the family produced saints is one thing; to make their other members nothing more than respectable worldly princes is quite another. The magnificent and magical figure of Alexander had once, for those who could accept it, a particular attraction. And only morons were repelled by it from the theory of the papacy. Romantics who were not morons were drawn to it precisely because of the theory of the papacy. Wicked bishops and wicked kings were common enough. But that the concentration of wickedness—avarice, pride, murder, incest—should exist in the See; that the infallible Vicar should possess the venom and be in love with his own uncanonical daughter; that that daughter should be throned in the Chair itself over adoring cardinals, and that the younger of her two brothers should assassinate the elder, and the awful three—the pontiff and the two children—should wind the world into their own skein of lust and cunning... this was the kind of thing that demanded the implicit presence of the whole future Roman development. The incarnation of Antichrist (romantically speaking) must be in the See of Christ. The scandal of the church had to be a scandal of the true church, or it lost half its lurid glory.

It seems it was not so. Lucrezia was less lovely and more moral than had been supposed, and Caesar, if as brilliant, was almost always excusable, and Alexander himself was no more than a great Renascence statesman, and it is most unlikely that he poisoned cardinals or even died of the venom himself; alas, only Christian rites took place in the pontifical chapels, even if the tapestries were a little pagan. The myth, however, had this to be said for it—it was contemporary. It was no more a late Protestant invention than the other legend of the Lady Joanna, Pontifex Maxima in the Dark Ages. It was accepted by pious and credulous chroniclers of the day. It was the kind of fable the Renascence liked, and it was enjoyed as a myth of that new discovery of the Renascence—*homo*, man.

It can hardly be said that the Middle Ages had neglected man. But then everything that the Renascence carried on was begun in the Middle Ages—science, art, scholarship, exploration. The Middle Ages paid their normal attention to the ordinary affairs of men, as all normal attention must be paid, *semper, ubique, ab omnibus.* When, however, they thought about those affairs, they imagined them in terms of God and grace. And eventually their energy could not live up to the dazzling circle of dogma within which it operated. God was everywhere the circumstance of all lives. Men had been over-nourished on such metaphysics, and the Renascence abandoned the idea of that universal Circumstance to attend to lesser circumstances. Change, sin, and intelligent delight in the creation had all been at work, and now they did not so much break bounds as withdraw from the bounds. The thought of the Middle Ages was not limited, but perhaps its philosophical vocabulary was.

Persistently and universally the stress changed. The lord Alexander VI was no worse than some of the medieval popes but he was—ever so little—different. He and Julius II and Leo X all accepted the Mass. But it is difficult to think of any of them as being primarily and profoundly concerned with the Mass. They were probably—even Julius—more humane than Urban VI but they were also more human. Urban was said to have read in his breviary while he listened to the moans and shrieks of the tortured cardinals; it would have been more characteristic of Alexander to have read pasquinades or love-songs while he caused to be poisoned—if he had done—his prisoner the lord Giambattista Orsini, cardinal-deacon of Santa Maria Nuova. Erasmus was as Christian as—and much less anti-papal (so to call it) than—Dante. But the monks, the heavy and certainly stupid monks, who denounced Erasmus were, in a sense, right. There was a great deal to be said for their point of view, though (as so often happens) they themselves were precisely the wrong people to say it. Erasmus can be studied and admired as a devout scholar. He can hardly be ranked as a scholarly devotee. Leonardo was probably a pious, if skeptical, scientist. But he could hardly be said, except in a highly mathematical manner, to exalt piety by science.

The opponents of either were no more pious or devout than scholarly or scientific. The habitual and rather worn religious intelligence of the time was not so high that it could afford to abuse Leonardo or Erasmus, as those periods might have done, with a better chance, to which grace was still a dreadful reality. "It is painful," wrote a later bishop,[1] "to sit and see and hear men arguing on the exigencies of the human race, and plainly ignorant of all that is passing in the head and heart, of that human race, beyond their own little fragment of it."

Meanwhile Machiavelli was writing about men. "We owe thanks," said Francis Bacon later, "to Machiavelli and to writers of his kind who openly and without dissimulation show what men are and not what they ought to be." Certainly Chaucer and Boccaccio had done much the same, but they had remembered what men ought to be. Machiavelli was a one-sided Augustinian; he laid open the secrets of man's natural corruption. It did not prevent his own large-minded honesty from being a simple Christian; it did allow him himself to be regarded as a myth of diabolical wickedness—only so far excusable that it was *homo* and not *homo-in-Deo* on which his eyes were observantly turned.

What, to such great men, was the vision of the glory of man in his capacious intellect, was in lesser men the vision of temporal and decorative glory, and in still lesser the vision of nothing much more than gold. Gold still for delight, for ornament, for display, as well as for possession, but still gold. The Middle Ages had desired greatness and glory and gold as much as their children; virtue after them was not so very much impaired. But the metaphysical vision which had illuminated those otherwise base things was passing; they were no longer mythological beyond themselves. Man was left to take glory in, and to glorify, himself and his works. Had chances been different, there might then have been a revival of the old wisdom of Christ as *anthropos* [man]; the secrets of Christendom might have enriched with new significance the material world. It was not to be; the *anthropos* had been forgotten for the *theos* [God], and now the other *anthropos*, the Adam of Augustine, the *homo sapiens* of science, preoccupied European attention.

But the *homo* was, at points, compacted and solidified. The Prince arose, and the separate princes. The rise of the nations had exalted those figures of surrounding kingship to more and more of a formal equality with their center the emperor. The Empire had been lost to Islam in the East; it was lost to Europe in the West. It was to linger there uncertainly till 1805, as in the East it was to be half-revived in Muscovy until 1917. The Great Schism had encouraged the thrones, for the decision between pontiff and pseudo-pontiff—the decision which of them was which, the decision which of them was canonically and righteously which, and where grace lay—had depended largely on the thrones. A hundred years had nearly passed, but the vibration lingered as the vibration of Napoleon lingers to-day. It lasted the longer because, by a natural impulse, the throne of Peter became one also among the thrones. The lord Alexander VI claimed, formally, to be sovereign over sovereigns; but his alliances and his armies and his treaties compelled him to be regarded as a prince by the princes. "The Lord Alexander VI was a very great man"[2]—so; but his manhood preoccupied the world more than his vicariate, and by an inevitable process both he and his allies and his opponents tended to regard Christ—in his church—as the Vicar of the Roman See rather than the Roman See as the Vicar of Christ. Messias was a province of the hierarchy and of the head of the hierarchy. It was but a part of the general change. Louis XI was even more superstitious than Louis IX but he was less supernatural. The emperor Maximilian had some thoughts of making himself pontiff, thoughts which would hardly have occurred to Saint Louis. The sacerdotal was a rank in the aristocracy, but the saintly had lost its appeal. It had ceased to be fashionable, and even when only fashionable sanctity has about it an energy in which the very fashions tremble. But now for awhile it was not much more than one of its own relics.

Homo, that is, had entered religion also. The cry of "Another is in me" had faded, and the Renascence glory was not attributed to the acts of that Other. Christ was encouraged, at need, to act the deeds of *homo;* hardly his own. At this particular moment in the history of Christendom acts had got largely out of hand. Faith (in Saint Paul's sense) was, no doubt, much practiced secretly but the most characteristic spectacular acts lacked its validity. The acts of a man without that validity tend to involve his lower nature more and more, and even the imaginative acts of the Renascence did not reach to "the top of speculation," except perhaps in the effort of Leonardo to measure the very angle of creation itself. The *Mona Lisa* is the effort of art to discover and pattern the very first creative movement of a smile; the whole superb labor of its painter discovered in creation the mathematical motion towards a similar ostentation. And even the vision of heart's peace so dear to Erasmus may have demanded for its full affirmation a second series of acts for which perhaps the great scholar knew his own incapacity.

The cry for reform which is always heard in the church was no less vocal then. It had always been admitted that a certain magnificence was becoming to the secular ritual of the church. Ritual and magnificence were now becoming vices, and the austere minds felt them so; nor was there discoverable, as so often there had been, a compensating energy in the convents and hermitages. Convents had become the subject of anxious consultation everywhere, which is not to say that they deserved it everywhere. But Another was no longer lucidly within their inhabitants; the lives which those inhabitants did not noticeably lay down for their brethren, as Clement of Alexandria had taught, attracted the attention of both better and worse men. The reforming party clamored, as always, for alteration, and were, as always, right. But because they were always clamoring and always right, no effective action was taken. They declaimed like the Communist leaders of our own day. They directed their attacks pointedly to the personal lives of the ecclesiastical officers. It is only of recent years that that personal attack has seemed to fail. Few Roman Catholics now denounce the secret vices of the pope; few Anglicans exhibit the loathsome corruption of their Archbishops; no president of any Free Church council is accused of sodomy or sloth. Perhaps indeed their lives are more pure, or perhaps vociferousness has merely exhausted itself.

Nevertheless a crisis approached, and the sublime discretion of our Lord the Spirit deigned to assist its production by the means of two characteristics of Christendom—exchange and conversion. As was said earlier, co-inherence had been the very pattern of Christendom; we were not to be merely inheritors but "brethren and fellows and co-inheritors of the name of salvation." And as Augustine had taught that that co-inherence stretched back to Adam, so Christendom had carried it forward and beyond into all relationships, up to the last point of the active blessed. The invocation of saints had arisen from it, and the practice of indulgences had defined it in action.

The first indulgences had been declared to the early crusaders; all temporal penalties of sin were remitted to those who fought. This was but a method, and two steps were still to be taken before the whole superb and dangerous knowledge became defined. In the thirteenth century Alexander of Hales defined the Treasury of Merits, and in 1343 the doctrine was accepted by Clement VI. In 1457 Calixtus III formally declared that the exercise of such powers was applicable beyond this world, so mightily had the organization become conscious of itself. It was indeed rather a new manner of measurement and a ratification which was then proclaimed, since prayer had always been believed to be effective in the divine will. But an accurate method of exchange was then presented to the faithful; by doing *this*, *that* would be achieved. Indulgences were "applicable to the souls in purgatory." Acts of love could be, definitely and locally, offered to the dead; the visible and invisible worlds co-inhered in that grace; the great means of substituted love became as visible on earth as it was in heaven. Money was, on earth, a means of artificial exchange, and could be, now, a means of the art of heavenly exchange—money given in repentance, in faith, in love. As the intention was struck into act—"as the money chinks in the box"—the effect was achieved—"the soul springs from purgatory."

It was, however, the chink of the money that too much deflected attention. The lord Leo X, acting within his pontifical rights and (by definition) offering the faithful a new opportunity of concrete and calculated exchange, and no less profitable to all souls concerned for being concrete and calculated, issued a special indulgence. That he wished to use the money obtained for building Saint Peter's was the lord Leo's own responsibility, and his own business how much piety went to the building. The arrangement made, however, did rather savor of simony. A particularly brilliant financial idea occurred to someone—to Leo, to a cardinal, to the archbishop of Mainz, or (since God frequently confounds his own works by the most unlikely instruments) to some clerk in the train of the archbishop or in the papal treasury at Rome who never perhaps lived to see the catastrophic results of his moment of commercial intelligence. The archbishop of Mainz, Albert of Hohenzollern, had just been elected. He was not yet of canonical age to hold a bishopric, and he already held two others—he was archbishop of Magdeburg and administrator of Halberstadt. He offered the pontiff ten thousand ducats for concession and confirmation. It was agreed that the money should be advanced by the great banking house of Fugger and paid to the pope, who should then allocate to Albert, for the Fuggers, the receipts from the indulgences. The Fuggers took over the management of the sale, arranged for commercial travelers—that is, preachers—sent agents with them to check the takings, and shared the results with the young archbishop. Such was the idea, such was the arrangement. Unfortunately whoever thought of it dropped a lighted match into that unknown cellar of man's mind which contains the heavily dynamic emotions known as "faith" and "works."

The sale was to begin from 1 April, 1515. Some six or seven years before, the second element in the approaching crisis had been prepared. A young monk of twenty-five or so, older by a year or two than the involved archbishop of Mainz, had found himself involved in another desire. His name was Luther; he was an Augustinian. Our Lord the Spirit permitted him to follow Augustine in Augustine's primary and continuous desire and to experience conversion. He labored for it; he suffered austerities, he read, he studied, he prayed, he agonized. He toiled under the teaching of William of Occam that salvation is (after grace) a matter of the will. It is conceivable that it was the later scholastics who were antipathetic to Luther; he liked Athanasius and read Augustine with passion. But all his duties, the sacrament and the solitary studies, brought him no help. The great organization of redemption coiled round him and his soul was in despair. "When I looked for Christ it seemed to me as if I saw the devil." A thousand years earlier the universe for Augustine had shifted its center in a garden; it did so suddenly now for Luther—it is said, on the Scala Sancta at Rome. In a passion of hopeless revolt against the will he had read the epistle to the Romans; he remembered suddenly "The just shall live by faith." He remembered; he stood up; all things swung into order. "The just shall live by faith." Faith.

It was not primarily the scholastics, however, but Aristotle who, he felt, had misled him and more enraged him—"that ridiculous and injurious blasphemer." "My soul longs for nothing so ardently as to expose and publicly shame that Greek buffoon, who like a specter has befooled the church." Aristotle had done nothing that he had needed, and brought no peace. He wrote to another Augustinian "You say with Israel: 'Peace, peace,' and there is no peace; say rather with Christ: 'Cross, cross,' and there is no cross. For the cross is no more a cross once you say joyously: 'Blessed cross, there is no tree like thee ...'" It was this experience which was setting him slowly at odds with his world—as for instance with the five thousand relics which the elector Frederick of Saxony kept in the castle church at Wittenburg, and with the theologians who stressed the language of "works."

In 1517 a traveling preacher of indulgences came near to Wittenburg; the Elector of Saxony had forbidden the sale to take place in his dominions, and the frontier was not crossed. The preacher was a Dominican named Tetzel; his work was assisted by the archbishop Albert who had announced in a declaration of the benefit of the indulgences that—at any rate for those applicable to the souls in purgatory: "Nor is it necessary for those who contribute to the fund for this purpose to be contrite or to confess." Tetzel preached enthusiastically; his hearers bought. In the miracle of co-inherence there is no reason to suppose that the indulgences were not effectual for all the glad and aspiring ghosts to whom they were offered. But of that assistance offered by the church militant to the church in purification the earthly scandal was an unfortunate result.

The tales told of Tetzel would be incredible were it not that the thing happening is so often more like a fable than the thing supposed. Luther, writing to the archbishop, said that people reported Tetzel as having preached that "there was no sin so great that it would not be absolved thereby, even if, as they say, taking an impossible example, a man should violate the mother of God. They believe that indulgences free them from all penalty and guilt." It is unlikely that Tetzel meant to commit himself to the heretical belief that an indulgence could free from *guilt*, as distinguished from the penalty. But it is not impossible that the crowd of German listeners understood him so, nor that his crude phrases may have risen to wild extravagances of rhetoric, carried off precisely by his choice of the impossible image of the *anthropotokos* [Mary] to particularize. Conceive a Shakespearian clown agitating for piety remote from the quiet studies of theologians, and the situation is credible. Tetzel afterwards denied most of the charges, believe him or not.

Even the broad taste of the times was a little shocked. Tetzel and the Fuggers' agents together were a little too much. The combination of a reckless oratory and a careful calculation were a little too—Shakespearian. Even so nothing might have happened if Luther had not been converted, "in the twinkling of an eye," to faith. He had known the Spirit. It had not entered his head to believe anything but that the organization of the church was at bottom actuated by the same Spirit. Yet his parishioners were full of the indulgences and not at all full of contrition. Contrition was not, in that age, a mark of the church. But it certainly had been a mark of Luther. He had been delivered into assurance. Neither contrition nor assurance, but an obscene parody of both, seemed to him encouraged by the click-clack of the money and the mechanism of grace. The machine had got out of control, through the faults of the hierarchy. He protested. He protested in the correct academic fashion. He put up theses for dispute; they were not extreme. He allowed "the apostolic truth of indulgences"; he said that "papal pardons are not to be despised." Nor did he produce any antagonistic theological doctrine. He protested, in fact, on the other side little that the calm thought of Christendom would not have admitted. But he did seem to reflect, if not, as Erasmus said later, on "the crown of the pope and the bellies of the monks," at least on the prestige of the pope and the profits of the preachers. The news of the protest spread; it reached the lord Leo, who was good natured, tolerant, amused. "A drunken German monk! he will think differently when he is sober!" Alas, the inebriation was deep; Luther had drunk of the intoxicating Blood.

Even now it seems astonishing that one moment, as against so many others, should have set fire to so much. Luther was neither a great mystic nor a great theologian. He might have found all that he ever found in a thousand orthodox doctors. He denied nothing, at least in the beginning, that a thousand orthodox doctors would not have denied. But two things combined against peace and reconciliation; the first was the immediate alignment of forces, the second was certain particular conversions permitted or encouraged by the Spirit.

The alignment of forces tended to be upon that old frontier of dispute, the argument on faith and works. It has often been regarded as a technicality of theology; in fact, of course, it is a matter like most theology—of everyday life. It is a matter of understanding and approach; it is almost a matter of style. Do we do best to think of achieving what we can by ourselves? or to rely upon something not ourselves? And if either, how far? and with what modifications? In such a matter as the desirability of loving A, do we leave it to X to love A? or do we try and love A directly? which is the best method for developing a pure style of love? We all know the deplorable false styles, the styles which say with intolerable arrogance "Oh well, I do what I can," or with an equally intolerable smirk "Oh well, of course, it isn't I that do it, but Something Else" (and if the Something Else is named the effect is no better). How do we become honest? and what kind of works does "faith" in love involve? Co-inherence is not finished with when it is named; how then do we best co-inhere?

High abstractions—upon which every minute of personal life depends! What is the nature of love? Christendom had felt how helpless man was to do anything; Paul and Augustine, to name no others, had become witnesses to *that*. You are no nearer being love because you have done acts of love. But are acts of love then of no account? Much every way, so long as you do not claim them for yours. But can I then not exist as action in love? Yes; you exist precisely, at fullest, in the acts which, most intensely, are not yours. And apart from them? Oh apart from them you are corrupt, lost, perishing everlastingly. Your acts are only from the fullness of the treasury of the all-meritorious love of God.

So, roughly, the Faith party; the Works took another, and parallel, line. You exist in those acts—yes; it is up to you to produce them. No one and nothing can produce them except you; unless you do, they will be everlastingly and eternally lost. They are of intense value; their value is such that they are not only applicable to the present situation but to all situations. They affect those dead long since and those yet unborn, as you are affected by the deeds of love of those not yet born or dead long since. All the sacraments are communications of love to all—through you. They at least are certain where so much is uncertain. Act then; act now; act, you. Work while it is called day. Without you and your acts—so marvelously has he limited himself that you may be co-inheritor with him—the acts of Love himself are not yet full.

The alternating stresses were reconcilable enough—in the hearts of the saints, the rhythms of Dante, or anyone's ordinary experience. Along both those parallel roads the columns of Christendom moved to take the kingdom of heaven by storm. But if the columns paused, quarrelled, turned hostile, faced each other, dug trenches along the ways? "The intellect," said Luther, "is the devil's whore." She may be, at least, the mistress of a passionate emotion, or she may indulge her own sensuality. But, to be fair to her, it is not only self-indulgence which drives her into controversies. Something has, in this world, to be said. It was all very well for the Incarnate Glory to refrain from defining his gospel, but he left the task to his disciples, and all the infallibilities have not yet succeeded in making it very much plainer. Saint Paul, it seems, was right; only the operation of "faith" succeeds.

At that moment there was, on the one side, a very high intellectual tradition, discovered by first-rate minds but then administered by fifth-rate. On the other side was a first-hand experience, preached largely by second-hand. On both sides were the tag-rag and bobtail of religion, and also the multitudes of the uncomprehending good. Between them were the humanists, the unfortunate intellectuals.

There was an unsatisfactory interview between Luther and the papal legate at Augsburg. There was a disputation at Leipzig, where Luther committed himself to the even more extreme (but ancient) view that general councils could err and had erred. The princes of Germany, a little put about by a tax that Leo proposed to lay on the states, for a crusade— about which everyone was very doubtful—were either lukewarm or hostile to the Italianate Roman See. In 1518 it became evident that Leo and Luther had each decided that the other was Antichrist. The bull of excommunication was issued in June; Luther in August replied with a volume on the Babylonish captivity of the church. The mitered splendors and the rituals of glory were beginning to seem to him very much like the pageanted gods of Assyria, and that fatal dream of a simple gospel was rising like a marsh-light over the too-soon-bloody swamp of Europe. Luther wrote to Erasmus, more or less suggesting an alliance. Erasmus replied much as Matthew Arnold might have replied to Wesley. He did not think either crowns or bellies worth war, but if war came he knew he would be found with the Roman See. But some of the younger humanists went over—notably, the almost equally quiet-loving Philip Melanchthon, who thus prepared for himself (like Newman later) a future of spiritual peace and temporal distress.

By 1520 bonfires—of books, so far—were taking place. The Papalists burnt Luther's and the Lutherans retaliated. Among the fires there appeared a fresh figure—the figure of the new emperor, Charles V. He had no extreme passion for humanism, though he admired it. He had no use at all for mystical conversion. He acknowledged the papacy, and he had a personal intention to see that the pope fitted in with his politics. He wished to restore the power of the Holy Roman Empire, and to be himself the Holy Roman Emperor. He was young, remote, practical, orthodox, and firm. He had no intention of assenting to heresy. Yet he was the first European sovereign who was compelled to exclude orthodoxy as a fundamental necessity in his subordinate sovereigns. He began in 1521 with the Diet of Worms. He was driven to compromise—*cujus regio ejus religio.*[3] Luther at Worms said "I can no other"; it was magnificent, but it was not politics.

After Worms Luther was secluded for some time in the Wartburg; he was there from May 1521 to March 1522. The dates recall the second condition which prolonged the split through the centuries. For from March 1522 to January 1523 Ignatius Loyola was also living in seclusion and devotion—but he at the cave of Manresa in Spain. In 1534, as a result of his

retirement Luther was able to publish the German translation
of the Bible. In the same year Ignatius with six companions
took the vows. Among the companions was Francis Xavier,
once a lecturer on Aristotle, converted and indoctrinated by
Ignatius. In the same year another young classical scholar, a
Frenchman who had published in 1532, with much applause,
a commentary on Seneca's *De Clementia* (strange choice!),
and had been living since in seclusion at Angoulême, also after conversion, composed a small treatise on the primal doctrines of Christianity. His name was John Calvin, and the
book was the first draft of the *Institutes of the Christian Religion*.

The German Bible, the Jesuits, the *Institutes*—all in one
year. And Luther, Ignatius, Xavier, Calvin—the dates of their
births are important, but those other dates of conversion are
much more important. In that great age of *homo*, with its
magnificence of scholarship, architecture, art, exploration,
war, its transient graces and terrene glories, it pleased our
Lord the Spirit violently to convulse these souls with himself.
Grace seized on those strategic centers for its own campaign.
It struck suddenly outward, as its most divine way is—since
the wise Pharisee collapsed outside Damascus—and now in a
German, a Frenchman, a Spaniard—and many others after
them. It had done so, often enough, in the Middle Ages, as
since; its business is always to restore contrition to man. But
now, when contrition, admitted as a theory, had largely disap-
peared as a fact, it renewed contrition. The awful conflict
opened with those separate vigils of conflict. Contrition had
been left, by the archbishop of Mainz in one set of indulgences, to the souls in purgatory, and he was technically correct. But the result was that, in the other set of indulgences,
for those living on earth, the need of contrition could hardly
be stressed. The rites of the church, however, even in that
age of *homo*, invoked Emmanuel. Her governors celebrated

them but did not preach their conditions—nor repentance, the greatest condition (save faith and charity) of all. They left it, at best, to be presupposed, and what was presupposed the Spirit gave the church again—or gave her Lord through her. They had professed contrition for their own purposes; they received contrition for his—"good measure, pressed down and running over." The champions of it and of its assurance—assurance by experience, assurance by belief—sprang into action. That they came as they did—hostile, militant, complete—was due precisely to the condition of sin in which Christendom had found itself and to the redemption which everlastingly works within her.

The tumult passed, inevitably, from souls to minds; minds commanded bodies; bodies took to weapons. The religious wars opened as formulation began. It centered at first on those old recurrent questions of the will, and the will in relation to grace, and grace in relation to the system. The great fundamental dogmas of the nature of Christ remained, in general, formally undisturbed. The Renascence had not attacked them; it had not been particularly aware of them. But it had been acutely aware of man's will, and of the glorious manifestations of man's will. In France and in Spain a more ancient experiment was again begun. Calvin and Loyola, cavalry commanders of the Spirit in the new campaign, sought also to discover man's will. But they sought its discovery in its supreme moment of self-destruction; they desired to compel it to say "My Eros is crucified." The same word sprang in both—*exercitus*, exercise, drill. *The Exercises* was the title of Loyola's manual; "this life is an exercise," wrote Calvin.

That those two masters should have been opposed was, humanly speaking, tragic. They were both children of Christendom, and of medieval Christendom, and at that a medieval Christendom illuminated by the earlier Fathers. They both maintained passionately the authority of the church. "We believe the church," wrote Calvin, "in order to have a certain assurance that we are members of it. For thus our salvation rests on firm and solid foundation, so that it cannot fall into ruin, though the whole fabric of the world should be dissolved," and he went on to quote Augustine. To say that Calvin was influenced by Augustine is a meiosis; Augustine is invoked on almost every page of the great *Institutes*. He says of him, in speaking of the great doctrine of election, "I need no words but his," and again, "I shall not hesitate to confess with Augustine: 'The will of God is the necessity of things.'"

It was this complete necessity which the genius of Calvin attempted to restore as the only basis of the universal church. He desired to attribute all initiative to God, and to show that all things existed only according to the will of that initiative. "Calvinism asks, with Lutheranism, that most pregnant of all questions: what shall I do to be saved? and answers it as Lutheranism answers it. But the great question that presses upon it is, How shall God be glorified?"[4] How but by acknowledging that in him alone is all decision? in him alone all necessity? in him alone all destination? He asserts, and we can but consent; we do it of necessity and yet voluntarily. We have chosen necessity, and that necessity elects as it will, some to salvation, some to damnation.

Augustine had said almost as much, and if it were not for Augustine's sweep of style even the "almost" would be exaggerated. But his great phrases soar above the very definitions they carry; Calvin quotes from him "We do not find grace by liberty, but liberty by grace." All the psychological doctors of the Mystical Way had assented. Calvin attempted to formulate that experience. But no such dogma has ever been satisfactory to the church that does not involve free lives mutually co-inhering, and necessity and freedom (dare one say?) mutually co-inhering. In the crucifixion of Messias necessity and freedom had mutually crucified each other, and both (as if in an exchanged life) had risen again. Freedom existed then because it must; necessity because it could. But Calvin crucified Adam upon Jesus; "Men are to be taught indeed that the Divine Benignity is free to all who seek it, without any exception." *But* "none begin to seek it but those who have been inspired by the Divine Grace." *All* initiative is from God.

Men have not, for the most part, been able to bear the terrible paradox of Calvin, and they have pretended that Calvinism is (intellectually) much easier than it is. They have in fact (though generally from mean motives of ignorance and dislike) brought it under the condemning sentence of Loyola: "We ought not to speak of grace at such length and so vehemently as to give rise to that poisonous teaching which takes away free will." But then Ignatius had a great advantage; he did not conceive himself to be laying down the first principles of the Christian religion, but only founding an order. He was no Calvin or Aquinas. He only sought to teach the soul to discover the personal will in its moment of destruction; he only immolated on a superhuman individual devotion the glory of the Renascence. He presumed man's personal freewill in heaven but he enlisted his followers to the loss of it on earth; so much so that the ecclesiastical authorities checked and modified the more extreme of his phrases. The constitution of his Society suggested a subordination to superiors of a more utter kind than Rome was prepared to allow. Even the famous phrase about black and white—"we ought always to believe that what seems to us white is black, if the hierarchical church so define it"—may allow of some discussion, though it is difficult to see in the end what other conclusion can be formally reached. What is clear is that here also contrition, election, annihilation, were living states. Newman defined the chief characteristic of Ignatius to be "prudence"—intelligence of the spirit. He, more than Calvin, exhibited (if he did not more believe) the doctrine of exchange.

Both those great men renewed the word. The sermon came again into its own, but more extremely under Calvin than under Ignatius. Of all the incomprehensibilities of that difficult time perhaps the most incomprehensible to us is the passion of the Reformed for sermons. That men and women should wish to sit and *listen*, to do nothing but sit and listen, for hours together, is unbelievable to us, and we explain it by thinking that they were listening for heresies, listening in fear of the power of the ministers, or listening in terrible delight to hear their enemies denounced to hell, and no doubt all these things sooner or later came in, but not one was the main thing; no, the main thing was simply the spoken word, the energy and accuracy of the spoken word, the salvation communicated in the sacrament of the spoken word. Those congregations returned almost to the "speaking with tongues" of an earlier day, though this speaking did not need interpretation, for the interpretation and the speaking were one. They returned to Pentecost and the Spirit manifesting by tongues. And besides the sermons there were other tongues—tongues of psalms and hymns and spiritual songs, but especially of psalms. Initiative of God, breath of the Spirit of God, words molded by the fiery Spirit from the burning hearts of his elect. "Praise him upon the loud cymbals; praise him upon the well-tuned cymbals." The cymbals were the voices; their sound went over the earth, and as the wars grew darker the noise grew fiercer.

"Let God arise, and let his enemies be scattered." Calvinist and Jesuit alike gave themselves to martyrdom, and the secular authorities labored to keep up with the intellectual rage that lit the fires, fires round the stake or fires under the gallows, fires of interior contrition catching and spreading, and changed into those other fires which should destroy the ungodly and make their very flesh the burning gate of hell for their souls, or image in their castrated bodies the sterile miseries of everlasting loss. "Let God arise, and let his enemies be scattered." The single spiritual conflicts of those great souls, those powers taking the kingdom by violence, and radiating their violence outward through Christendom, opened into a general temporal conflict. Noise and austerity went with them; their high rage of righteousness drew armies after them, and the agony of a wailing continent replied to their silent agonies of attention. The real reformation, of which the Reformation generally so-called is but a small part, advanced. But as it came "let God arise and let his enemies be scattered"—it too much lost the thoughts of co-inherent love. Contrition indeed was renewed—but not for its own day, only for the day before yesterday.

Endnotes

1. Bishop Ullathorne, 2 July, 1870. *The Vatican Council*, Dom Cuthbert Butler.

2. *The House of Borgia*, F. Rolfe (called Baron Corvo).

3. The local religion is to be that of the local ruler; literally, "whose the region, his the religion." [C.H.]

4. *Calvin and Calvinism*, Benjamin Warfield.

SENSUALITY AND SUBSTANCE

This essay, published in *Theology* (May 1939) is one of several Williams wrote on the theme of the holiness of matter. It takes the form of reflections on D.H. Lawrence, but begins, typically, with Julian of Norwich and ends with the Athanasian Creed and the Ascension of Christ.

For I saw full assuredly, wrote the Lady Julian, "that our Substance is in God, and also I saw that in our sensualite God is; for in the self point that our Soul is made sensual, in the self point is the City of God ordained to Him from without beginning; into which seat He cometh and never shall remove it...and as anent our substance and sensualite it may rightly be cleped our soul: and that is because of the oneing that they have in God. The worshipful City that our Lord Jesus sitteth in is our sensualite, in which He is enclosed: and our kindly Substance is enclosed in Jesus with the blessed Soul of Christ sitting in rest in the Godhead."

Whatever the Lady Julian meant by "sensualite," she certainly meant nothing less material or less vital than the whole physical nature; she was not weakening or refining it away. She followed the church, which, ever since it had rejected the Nestorian idea of a merely moral union of the two natures in

Christ, had been committed to a realistic sense of the importance of matter: "our soul with our body, and our body with our soul, either of them taking help of other," which is not Browning but the Lady Julian again. The operations of matter are a means of the operation of Christ, and the body has not, in fact, as some pious people suggest, fallen a good deal farther than the soul.

This is all elementary enough; it is implicit or explicit in all the rites and all the rituals. It remains, however, that the help which the body gives to the soul has been far less seriously examined than the help which the soul gives to the body. The dichotomy which orthodoxy turned out of its official dogma has continually returned in its unofficial language; the result was epigrammatized in the question of Patmore's daughter: "Father, isn't marriage rather a wicked sacrament?" The Way of the Rejection of Images has been far more considered throughout Christendom than the Way of the Affirmation of Images—unless, indeed, those images were of the accepted religious kind. Yet the two ways have the same maxim and the same aim—"to love everything because God loves it." This is their union, and, this laid down, one way is not superior to the other, nor perhaps more difficult.

The result of our unofficial Manichaeism has been that when the official representatives of the church have talked about such things as sexual love (to take one example), they may have said the right things, but they have said very few of them and they have generally said them in the wrong style. The great world and energy of the body have been either deprecated or devotionalized; and by devotionalized I mean turned into a pale imitation of "substance," of spirit; thus losing their own powers and privileges without, in general, gaining any others. There has been a wide feeling that the more like an indeterminate soul the body can be made the better. But the *anthropos* in Christ was not "like" the *theos:* it was like nothing but itself. So the body is not "like" the soul; it is like nothing but itself. The principle of our sensuality is unique and divine. It is, no doubt, rooted in substance. "Soul is form and doth the body make" is a fine Platonist line. But soul ought not to be allowed to reduce the body to its own shadow—at any rate, in the Christian church.

The result of this shy spiritualism has been, of course, to leave the church particularly open to attack, or rather to leave its general public particularly open to attack. The church owes more to heretics than she is ever likely (on this earth) to admit; her gratitude is always slightly patronizing. There existed, in the early part of the twentieth century, a convinced and rhetorical heretic named David Herbert Lawrence. Of what exactly he was convinced it is not always easy to be sure, except on the very broadest lines. He thought that sex was important; he thought physical nature significant; he thought modern industrialism disgusting; he thought men needed leaders—or a leader; he thought also that each man must find out his own foundations, leader or no leader. His style as a leader was much more like Luther or Wesley than Calvin or Aquinas. But on quite a number of occasions he knew how to use words, and he produced for some time a very great effect on sections of the general public. This was accentuated by the suppression of some of his books and pictures by the state, which excited a number of the young to something like a sexual frenzy on Lawrence's behalf, and also cordially interested on his behalf a number of the more mature.

When Lawrence died, at the age of forty-five, in 1930, a number of books were written about him by his friends. This fortune, good or bad, he shared with others. Men and women who had known him wrote about him and about themselves; quite properly, for the only way in which they could explain his effect on them was by writing about themselves. But his capacity and effect as a writer were there subordinated to his personality. That some of the books which appeared should seem to deal too much with the difficulties and disputes between his friends was inevitable; a little spite could not be kept out and a little superiority was eagerly invited in. These things fade; the really interesting question is whether and to what extent Lawrence will fade. Even now, that seems almost impossible to anyone who remembers the thunder of the captains and the shouting; the first reading of the full version of *Lady Chatterley's Lover*, its moving beauty, its increasing repetitions; or the half-jest, half-assent with which one heard of the "dark gods"—dimly recollecting at the same time the fiery darkness of Boehme or the monstrous fables of the alchemical design.

He convinced only partly by his own language, and partly by his readers' memories—by that and by the sense of the blood, by that and by the sense of poetry. He could not be regarded as a serious poet, though he wrote some good poems. But he had a power to arouse, without any specially memorable phrase, a chaotic sense of poetic images. These certainly could not be even partially analyzed; they were of the same kind as those in Blake's *Prophetic Books*—gigantic and cloudy, unlike the mighty but lucid powers of Milton. And this was accentuated by the tendency of his confused mind to denounce, on behalf of the blood, the graces of intelligence, the holy intellect itself. It is not surprising that he should dislike all that he could understand of Jane Austen, but that he should prefer the "blood-stream" in Defoe or Fielding, because there was more "character" in them and less "personality"—this is a little odd. He thought, no doubt, he was protesting again, in literature, against the weakening of the style, but it was not so; only the richness of Jane Austen did not have to shout its sensuality aloud.

He was greatly moved also by the notion of authority. It seems sometimes that he was chiefly moved by the notion that he was himself authority—and yet he fled from that as much as he turned to it. To judge by his *Letters,* it was the war of 1914-18 which drove him into an antagonism to his kind, and provoked (as it very naturally might) a sense of separation and therefore—in him—of superiority. Against that sense of superiority, nevertheless, he was always reacting, partly from fear, partly from intelligence, partly from (what is the same thing) humility. He knew that authority comes into action only by "a dark unfathomable free submission." Of that kind of submission he saw no sign in the world around him— neither in the mining-village of his birth, nor in the scholastic world of his teaching days, nor in the intellectual circles of his later life. "Grace does not come through liberty, but liberty through grace," Calvin quoted from Augustine, and Lawrence might have quoted it from either, had he been fortunate enough to know either. He felt that great truth by nature, but he could not find its vocabulary. He felt desperately the cheapening all round him of words, of sex, of life. And he conceived (like the church) that the redemption lay in something other than morals—however important morals might be, and he was not one to cheapen them. At the end of *Aaron's Rod,* after pages of discussion, he wrote a few sentences which achieve their effect partly by being *there*—at the end:

> There was a long pause. Then Aaron looked up into Lilly's face. It was dark and remote-seeming. It was like a Byzantine eikon at the moment.
>
> "And whom shall I submit to?" he said.
>
> "Your soul will tell you," replied the other.

He stopped—most fortunately—there. He could not always stop; he was unlike a Byzantine eikon in that. An insensitiveness to his medium sometimes accompanied his ill-defined gospel; the two inadequacies are related. He would—and did—break off the story of a perfectly good dinner-party to go off, like Thackeray, into a long disquisition. But unlike Thackeray, he has not both his methods on one level, so that the reader is made almost physically ill by the jerk. It is not altogether a matter of his too-often irritated language, for his irritation produced at times the most healthy comments. Few sentences can be more urgently recommended to many Christian writers than: "You want to whoosh off in a nice little love-whoosh and lose yourself." God, it has been said, loves himself as the Good and not as himself, and love must in general be an act of the will. But Lawrence was aware, in those around him, of love as a poor emotionalism, and of the will as a dry sectarian thing. He fled from such sterilities and liquidities to the power from which they seemed to have been abstracted, to the depths of "sensualite" and the aeonian process of the blood.

Mr. Hugh Kingsmill's study of him is a biography, and carefully not much more than a biography. It ought to serve that purpose for some years, for it must be practically the only book on Lawrence uncolored by personal acquaintance or intellectual approval or disapproval of its subject's varied views. Mr. Kingsmill has his views, of course, but he tries not to press them unduly and he subdues the natural amusement or unhappiness which some of Lawrence's relations with his acquaintances provoke. "They filch my life for a sensation to themselves," he said in one of his letters, and it was not altogether untrue; their books show it. But it may be added on their side that it was precisely sensation which he offered them and which he professed to be valid. "The phallic consciousness," he wrote, "is not the cerebral sex-consciousness, but something really deeper, and the root of poetry, lived or sung." Certainly a cerebral sex-consciousness is not likely to be the root of much poetry, but then neither is the phallic consciousness unless some kind of cerebralism assists it. Dante asserts that when he first saw Beatrice the spirits of his sensations, of his emotions, and of his intellect were all stirred at once. The first exclaimed: "Ah wretch! how often I shall be hampered henceforth!"; the second: "Behold a god mightier than I who is come to rule over me!"; the third: "Now your beatitude has appeared." Dante spent a good deal of the rest of his life finding out what exactly they meant. But much as Dante may rebuke Lawrence, he is no less of a rebuke to those who attempt to annex poetry ("lived or sung"— whatever that means) to a spiritualism of sensibility. Poetry is sensual and intellectual—like sex. Both have, as Wordsworth said, "a strength of usurpation," and Wordsworth went on to say that in that usurpation

> *When the light of sense*
> *Goes out, but with a flash that has revealed*
> *The invisible world, doth greatness make abode,*
> *There harbours.*

It is the vast union of visible and invisible, tangible and intangible, which is the real business of exploration—anyhow for Christians. The Christians of Lawrence's day did not care for the exploration of the body; he reacted against them with a natural but undesirable violence. Mr. Ford Madox Ford has said: "Lawrence had the misfortune to become conscious of life in London and in a class in London that by a sort of inverted Puritanism insisted that a sort of nebulous glooming about sex was a moral duty and a sort of heroism." But the Christians had driven them to it by a kind of nebulous gilding of sex and the body; they had refined the body into an unreal phantom of dim light and called it the resurrection. Their morals aimed at a docetic Christ, and the awful creeds recalled them in vain.

Mr. Kingsmill's enjoyable book should be accompanied by Mr. Aldous Huxley's introduction to the *Letters,* for that presents convincingly the effect of Lawrence's personality on his friends—in a way that others (say Mabel Dodge's *Lorenzo in Taos)* do not. Mr. Huxley quotes Vernon Lee as saying: "He sees more than a human being ought to see," and he adds, "To be with him was to find oneself transported to one of the frontiers of human consciousness." He goes on to say: "He could cook, he could sew, he could darn a stocking and milk a cow, he was an efficient wood-cutter and a good hand at embroidery, fires always burned when he laid them and a floor, after Lawrence had scrubbed it, was thoroughly clean." Mr. Kingsmill tells the story of his crying out, in a car which had broken down, and of the mechanics of which he knew nothing: "I am a failure! I am a failure as a man in a world of men!" Obviously, it was not true. He was a man, he was a writer, he might have been a leader—had he had any idea of precisely where to lead or exactly how, had he heard of the way of Affirmation of Images.

Of that way he was inevitably ignorant. Nor, it seems, did he find any satisfactory other. As a prophet, therefore, he was something of a failure, but, to do him justice, it was a role which he never desired. Unfortunately, the imposed vocation interfered with another authority which he did half-acknowledge, the authority of the English language. He could do things with it, he did them too rarely. He did create a few human emotions; he occasionally achieved something almost non-human. The end of *The Woman Who Rode Away* invokes a strange unworldly landscape and action—except for the last sentence or two when some merely silly remark walks solemnly in. He did it in *Kangaroo* and *The Plumed Serpent—* the edge of an inhuman greatness rises on the horizon, and he attempts violently to invoke it, or he reproves us for not knowing it—and it is gone at once. The short stories have sometimes a human, sometimes an inhuman, effect. He tried occasionally the modern style of having no particular effect at all—a thing which lesser people did better.

The same difficulty, the same uncertainty, hover over his efforts at more familiar things. He knew about the world of *Sons and Lovers,* but neither he nor his readers know about the monotonously boring world of "passion" (passion!) in *The Trespassers.* But perhaps he never came nearer to the actuality of what he thought he was writing about and wanted to write about than in a sentence in *The White Peacock:* "The soft outstretching of her hand was like the whispering of strange words into the blood, and as she fingered a book the heart watched silently for the meaning." The wonder, the intense awareness of *meaning,* in such a hand, or in any other such member of the physical body, the moment of great expectation of great wisdom, was the moment he greatly desired to explore. He believed that there was meaning, and his sincerity was in that unresting desire. He wandered round the world seeking it; he blamed Europe, and Asia, and America, for not giving it to him. "Yet I don't believe in Buddha—hate him in fact—his rat-hole temples and his rat-hole religion. Better Jesus." The phrase was more accurate than he, ignorant of Christianity, knew. But for reasons the disciples of Jesus whom he did know were incapable of explaining. They had not attended to the Athanasian Creed. Yet that great ode contains in itself much that Lawrence might have recognized. It does not insist, as he sometimes did, that one must be *oneself,* that one must be *alone.* With probably a greater justice than his, it may be supposed to assume that most people, somehow or other, discover that they are alone all too painfully, and as for being oneself...But it does insist precisely on what he was always emphasizing: that the life of "sensuality" and the life of "substance" cannot be separated and must not be confused.

> For as the reasonable soul and flesh is one man; so God and
> Man is one Christ.
> One, not by conversion of the Godhead into flesh, but by
> taking of the manhood into God.
> One altogether, not by confusion of substance, but by unity
> of Person.

If this is so, we may have to recover for all that creation
the Way of the Affirmation of its Images. We shall take no
harm from it; we need not be morally nervous; its difficulties
are no more, though certainly no less, than the difficulties of
the Way of the Rejection of Images which, on the whole, the
Christian notabilities have so far preferred. The movements
for housing and social reform, the consciousness of the dispossessed masses, have already prepared the way as an accident of their own preoccupation. There is no likelihood that
we shall become more amorously promiscuous because the
other preoccupation is heartened by the physical intellect, because we have more meaning to brood over. The great identity of the *anthropos* will be preserved the better in the
categories of substance and sensuality the more we attend to
those categories as such. The *New Life* of Dante does not begin to talk *only* of the spirit; no, that young and great doctor
faints at the sight of his beloved; he cries when she cuts him;
he is like any hysterical adolescent—that is, like anyone much
in love. And the great surge of passion that immortally follows is precisely not a passion in which sensuality is refined
away; at the close of the *Purgatory* she says to him: "You
should have been faithful to my buried flesh," *mia carne se-
polta*, and in her actual eyes he sees reflected the two-natured
gryphon of Christ. There is no intenser image of the whole
business of Romantic Theology—if it may so be called, meaning by the words that kind of theology which devotes itself to
the serious study of the great romantic movement such as
Dante and Wordsworth knew (in their separate kinds). It is

Dante's image of "the self point of union" where is the City; it is the flash of the sudden usurpation of flesh which reveals the greatness of the invisible City.

The wonder, the thrill, of a shoulder or a hand awaits its proper exploration. At present we have simply nothing to say to anyone in a state of exaltation, watching for "meaning," except something which sounds very much like: "Well, don't look too intently." The hungry sheep look up for metaphysics, the profound metaphysics of the awful and redeeming body, and are given morals. Yet they are encouraged to receive the Blessed Sacrament which is defined to be for the body and the soul. Lawrence was a heretic—good; but he was concerned with a Christian orthodoxy—the orthodoxy of the blood of man.

How to discover that? God knows; it cannot be done in study circles. We might certainly consider what has been done—there is the Lady Julian, there is Dante, there are Donne and Patmore. There is Lawrence. It is urgent that we should do it; it is even more urgent that we should not be ingenious and that we should take care of our style. Lawrence asserted that "we shall never free the phallic reality from its 'uplift' taint till we give it its own phallic language and use the obscene words." He was certainly wrong, but he was no more wrong than those who habitually use a vocabulary which completely consists of uplift. For the result of that kind of evasion of "sensuality" is the destruction of "substance." The only "uplift" permissible is that of the Ascension, and it was a real body (the very root of all sensuality) which there withdrew through all the dimensions. "Handle me and see—." Repulsive materialism! But that was how the divine Word talked.

THE INDEX of the BODY

As published in the *Dublin Review* (July 1942) this essay suffered from some editorial censorship. For her collection of Williams's essays, *The Image of the City*, Anne Ridler was able to restore the excisions from his manuscript, and her version is printed here.

In the *Prelude* (book 8, ll. 279-81) Wordsworth wrote:

> *the human form*
> *To me became an index of delight,*
> *Of grace and honour, power and worthiness.*

The most important word there is *index*. There are moments in all poetry when the reader has to ask himself whether a word used by the poet is accurate not only for the poet's universe but for the reader's own. It is a secondary decision, since the first must be only of the poetic value, but it is sometimes important. That is so here; the word *index*, pressed to its literal meaning, is a word which demands attention, and afterwards assent or dissent.

It is true that Wordsworth himself did not develop the idea; he is speaking generally, and in other passages his genius suggests that the index is to a volume written in a strange language. This is no weakness in Wordsworth; it was, on one side, his particular business. Thus the image of the Leech-Gatherer in *Resolution and Independence* is drawn at least as inhuman as human; so is the Soldier in book 4 of the *Prelude* who is the cause of such terror, and the other wanderers; the woman with the pitcher, and even Lucy Gray, are of the same kind. They are on the borders of two worlds, which almost pass and repass into each other. Wordsworth, of all the Romantics, came nearest to defining and mapping that borderland.

There are, of course, also his more exclusively human figures—Michael, for instance, in the poem of that name. Here the human form suggests to him the grandeur of the moral virtues; it is the suffering and laboring spirit of man which he sees. That may have been what he had chiefly in mind in the passage I have quoted: man as "a solitary object and sublime," but man also "with the most common; husband, father," who

> *suffered with the rest*
> *From vice and folly, wretchedness and fear.*

But the passage is capable of another reading, and one which proposes to us a real, if less usual, sequence. It is that reading which I wish now to discuss, and the word *index* is the beginning. The question proposed is whether we shall take that word seriously as a statement of the relation of the human form to "grace and honor, power and worthiness." The human form meant, to Wordsworth, the shape of the shepherd seen among the hills. There it was high and distant. It was a whole being significant of a greater whole—which is, in some sense, the definition of objects seen romantically. But the lines might be applied to the same shape, seen near at hand and analytically. They might refer to the body itself; it is that which can be considered as an index.

What then would be meant by the word? Nothing but it-self. An index is a list of various subjects, with reference to those places where, in the text of the volume, they are treated at greater length. But, at least, the words naming the subjects are the same; and a really good index will give some idea of the particular kind of treatment offered on the separate pages. Some such idea, Wordsworth's lines suggest, the body and even the members of the body may give of the delight, grace, honor, power, and worthiness of man's structure. The structure of the body is an index to the structure of a greater whole.

I am anxious not to use words which seem too much to separate the physical structure from the whole. The fact of death, and the ensuing separation of "body" and "soul," lead us to consider them too much as separate identities con-joined. But I hope it is not unorthodox to say that body and soul are one identity, and that all our inevitable but unfortu-nate verbal distinctions are therefore something less than true. Death has been regarded by the Christian church as an outrage—a necessary outrage, perhaps, but still an outrage. It has been held to be an improper and grotesque schism in a single identity—to which submission, but not consent, is to be offered; a thing, like sin, that ought not to be and yet is. The distress of our Lord in his passion may perhaps not improp-erly be supposed to be due to his contemplation of this all but inconceivable schism in his own sacred and single iden-tity. If our manhoods were from the first meant indivisibly, how much more his!

It is one of the intellectual results of the Fall that our lan-guage has always to speak in terms of the Fall; and that we cannot help our language does not make it any more true. The epigrams of saints, doctors, and poets, are the nearest we can go to the recovery of that ancient validity, our unfallen speech. To treat the body as an index is to assume that, as in an index the verbal element—the *word* given—is the same as in the whole text, so in the physical structure of the greater index the element—the *quality* given—is the same as in the whole structure. Another poet, Patmore, put the thing in a similar light when he wrote that

> *from the graced decorum of the hair,*
> *Ev'n to the tingling sweet*
> *Soles of the simple earth-confiding feet*
> *And from the inmost heart*
> *Outwards unto the thin*
> *Silk curtains of the skin,*
> *Every least part*
> *Astonish'd hears*
> *And sweet replies to some like region of the spheres.*

"The spheres" there are likely to mean, first, the outer heavens. This idea is practically that of the microcosm and the macrocosm: the idea that a man is a small replica of the universe. Man was "the workshop of all things," "a little world," *mundus minor exemplum majoris mundi ordine, filius totius mundi.*[1] It is a very ancient idea; it was held before Christianity and has been held during Christianity; it was common to Christians, Jews, and Mohammedans; and, for all I know, the scientific hypothesis of evolution bears a relation to the union of the two. Into that, however, I am not learned enough to go.

The idea went through many changes, but its general principle remained constant: that man was the rational epitome of the universe. It led, of course, to many absurdities, and (if you choose—like any other idea) to some evils. Some writers catalogued painstakingly the more obvious fantasies: hair was the grass or the forests; bones were mountains; the sun was the eyes, and so on. Astrology, if not based on it, at least found the idea convenient; however we may reject that ancient study, it had at least this philosophic principle mixed up with it—that each man, being unique, was a unique image of the universe, that the spatially greater affected the spatially lesser, and the calculable influences of the stars were only calculable because each man represented and reproduced the whole. Astrology then was a high and learned science; it was forbidden for good reasons, but it was not fatalistic. It did not say "this will certainly happen"; it said: "Given these stellar and individual relations, this result is likely." But the will of God and the wills of men were allowed much freedom to interfere with the result. *Sapiens dominabitur astris.*[2] The paragraphs in our papers today bear as much resemblance to the science as texts lifted up on boards outside churches do to the whole dogmas of the church. The paragraphs are, I allow, more likely to harm; the texts, on the whole, are innocuous.

Beside, or rather along with, this study went the patterns of other occult schools. The word "occult" has come into general use, and is convenient, if no moral sense is given it simply as itself. It deals with hidden things, and their investigation. But in this case we are concerned not so much with the pretended operations of those occult schools as with a certain imagination of relation in the universe, and that only to pass beyond it. The signs of the zodiac were, according to some students, related to the parts of the physical body. The particular attributions varied, and all were in many respects arbitrary. But some of them were extremely suggestive; they may be allowed at least a kind of authentic poetic vision. Thus, in one pattern, the house of the Water-carrier was referred to the eyes; the house of the Twins to the arms and hands; the house of the Scorpion to the privy parts and the sexual organs; and the house of the Balances to the buttocks.

It will be clear that these four attributions at least had a great significance. It will be clear also that in such a poetic (so to call it) imagination, we are dealing with a kind of macrocosmic-microcosmic union of a more serious and more profitable kind than the mere exposition by a debased astrology of chances in a man's personal life. It may be invention, but if so, it is great invention; the houses of the zodiac, with their special influences ruling in special divisions of the spatial universe, may be but the fables of astronomy; it must be admitted that few certain facts support them. But they are not unworthy fables. They direct attention to the principles at work both in the spatial heavens and in the structure of man's body. Aquarius is for water, clarity, vision; Gemini are for a plural motion, activity, and achievement; Libra is for that true strength of balance on which the structure of man depends.

With this suggestion, we are on the point of deserting the spatial heavens for something else. The like regions of the spheres, of which Patmore spoke, here begin to be transferred to the spiritual heavens. "As above, so below" ran the old maxim, but even that dichotomy is doubtful. The houses of the zodiac, in this, do but confuse the issue, except in so far as they, like the whole universe, exhibit the mystery by which spirit becomes flesh, without losing spirit. Perhaps the best verbal example is in the common use of the word "heart." Even in our common speech the word is ambiguous. To call Hitler heartless means that he seems to be without the common principle of compassion. It is said that Tertullian (but I have not found the reference) said that "the supreme principle of intelligence and vitality," "the sovereign faculty" of man, resided "where the Egyptians taught—*Namque homini sanguis circumcordialis est sensus*, the sense of man is in the blood around the heart." At least the pulsating organ presents, for man, his proper physical rhythm in the whole—

mundus minor exemplum majoris mundi ordine. As our meaning—physical life or compassionate life—so the word heart. Compassion is the union of man with his fellows, as is the blood. The permitted devotion to the Sacred Heart is to the source of both. The physical heart is, in this sense, an "index" to both. Gerard Hopkins wrote, of the Blessed Virgin:

> *If I have understood*
> *She holds high motherhood*
> *Towards all our ghostly good*
> *And plays in grace her part*
> *About man's beating heart,*
> *Laying, like air's fine flood,*
> *The deathdance in his blood*
> *Yet no part but what will*
> *Be Christ our Saviour still.*

The visionary forms of the occult schools are but dreams of the divine Body.

All these brief allusions show that there have been some traditions of significance—poetic, occult, religious. Christians, however, may be permitted to press the significance more closely; they may be allowed to ask whether the body is not indeed a living epigram of virtue. There have been doctors who held that Christ would not have become incarnate if man had not sinned; there have been doctors who held that he would. Either way, it is clear that the sacred Body was itself virtue. The same qualities that made his adorable soul made his adorable flesh. If the devotion to the Sacred Heart does not, in itself, imply something of the sort, I do not know what it does imply.

The virtues are both spiritual and physical—or rather they are expressed in those two categories. This is recognized in what are regarded as the more "noble" members in the body—the heart, the eyes. But it is not so often recognized as a truth underlying all the members—the stomach, the buttocks. That is partly because we have too long equated the body as such with the "flesh" of Saint Paul. But "flesh" is no more that than [...] it is "sex." The body was holily created, is holily redeemed, and is to be holily raised from the dead. It is, in fact, for all our difficulties with it, less fallen, merely in itself, than the soul in which the quality of the will is held to reside; for it was a sin of the will which degraded us. "The evidence of things not seen" is in the body seen as this epigram; nay, in some sense, even "the substance of things hoped for," for what part it has in that substance remains to it unspoiled.

It is in this sense then that the body is indeed an "index" to delight, power, and the rest. "Who conceives," wrote Prior,

> *Who conceives, what bards devise*
> *That heaven is placed in Celia's eyes?*

Well, no; not so simply as that. But Celia's eyes are a part of the body which (said Patmore, who was orthodox enough)

> *Astonish'd hears*
> *And sweet replies to some like region of the spheres.*

And those spheres are not merely the old spatial macrocosmic heavens, but the deep heaven of our inner being. The discernment of pure goodwill, of (let it be said for a moment) pure love in Celia's eyes, at some high moment of radiant interchange or indeed at any other moment, is no less part of the heavenly vision (so tiny and remote as it may be) because it is a physical as well as a spiritual vision. The word "sacramental" has perhaps here served us a little less than well; it has, in popular usage, suggested rather the spiritual *using* the physical than a common—say, a single—operation.

Eyes then are compacted power; they are an index of vision; they see and refer us to greater seeing. Nor has the stomach a less noble office. It digests food; that is, in its own particular method, it deals with the nourishment offered by the universe. It is a physical formula of that health which destroys certain elements—the bacteria which harmfully approach us. By it we learn to consume; by it therefore to be, in turn, consumed. So even with those poor despised things, the buttocks. There is no seated figure, no image of any seated figure, which does not rely on them for its strength and balance. They are at the bottom of the sober dignity of judges; the grace of a throned woman; the hierarchical session of the pope himself reposes on them: into even greater images and phrases we need not now go.

It will be thought I labor the obvious; and I will not go through the physical structure suggesting and propounding identities. The point will have been sufficiently made if the sense of that structure being heavenly not by a mere likeness but in its own proper nature is achieved. It is a point not so much of doctrine as of imagination. That imagination is at once individual and social. The temples of the Holy Ghost are constructed all on one plan: and our duties to our material fellows are duties to structures of beatitude. The relation of the Incarnation to our own mode of generation is blessedly veiled. But its relation to those other identities of power is not at all doubtful. It is not only physical structures we neglect or damage by our social evils; it is living indexes of life. The virtues exist in all of them materially, but it is the virtues which so exist. Christ, in some sense, derived his flesh from them, for he derived it from his mother, and she from her ancestors, and they from all mankind.

The sacred Body is the plan upon which physical human creation was built, for it is the center of physical human creation. The great dreams of the human form as including the whole universe are in this less than the truth. As his, so ours; the body, in this sense of an index, is also a pattern. We carry about with us an operative synthesis of the Virtues; and it may be held that when we fall in love (for example), we fall in love precisely with the operative synthesis.

> *Grace was in all her steps, heaven in her eye;*
> *In every gesture dignity and love;*

is much more a definite statement of fact than we had supposed; footsteps are astonishing movements of grace. That we cannot properly direct and control our sensations and emotions is not surprising; but the greatness of man is written even in his incapacity, and when he sins he sins because of a vision which, even though clouded, is great and ultimate. As every heresy is a truth pushed disproportionately, so with every sin; at least, with every physical sin. But, however in those states of "falling in love" the vision of a patterned universe is revealed to us, the revelation vanishes, and we are left to study it slowly, heavily, and painfully. All that the present essay attempts to do is to present a point of view which has behind it, one way and another, a great tradition—a tradition which, for Christians, directs particular attention to the sacred Body as the archtype of all bodies. In this sense the eucharist exposes also its value. The "index" of our bodies, the incarnate qualities of the moral universe, receive the archtype of all moralities truly incarnated; and not only the pattern in the soul and will but the pattern in the body is renewed. Or, better, in that unity which we, under the influence of our Greek culture, divide into soul and body. Dr. William Ellis writes,

> Socrates invented the concept which permeates every part of modern thinking, the concept of the twofold nature of man, of man as a union of the active, or spiritual, with the inactive, or corporeal; the concept, in short, of the organism as a dead carcass activated by a living ghost. Even if we repudiate this idea, we are still half-dominated by it, so deeply does it underlie our pattern of culture.[3]

CHARLES WILLIAMS

I am far from suggesting that this is the proper Christian view. But there is, I think, no doubt that it is not far from the popular Christian view. The fuss that has been made about Browning's line (not that that was Browning's fault)—"nor soul helps flesh more now than flesh helps soul"—shows that. It was repeated almost as a new revelation, though indeed the Lady Julian had said almost the same thing centuries before. We have to overcome that lazy habit of the imagination—the outrage of death notwithstanding. We experience, physically, in its proper mode, the kingdom of God: the imperial structure of the body carries its own high doctrines—of vision, of digestion of mysteries, of balance, of movement, of operation. "That soul," said Dante in the *Convivio*, "which embraces all these powers [the rational, the sensitive, and the vegetative] is the most perfect of all the rest." The rational, or self conscious, power is indeed the noblest, but we must ask from it a complete self-consciousness, and not a self-consciousness in schism.

It was suggested that the stress of this imagination may be an incentive to our social revolution. For if the body of our neighbor is compact of these heavenly qualities, incarnated influences, then we are indeed neglecting the actual kingdom of God in neglecting it. It is the living type of the Arch-typal. We have not merely to obey a remote moral law in feeding and succoring and sheltering it. It is the "index" of power; tear away the index, and we are left without the power; tear away the index, and we are left without the delight. Let the whole to which that index witnesses be as immense as any volume of truth may be, and still the value of that small substance remains. Every student of a learned work uses the index attentively. A good index can indeed be studied in itself. To study the body so is to increase our preparation for the whole great text.

Endnotes

1. "A lesser world, in its order an example of a greater world, and child of the whole world." [C.H.]

2. "The wise person will have dominion over the stars." [C.H.]

3. *The Idea of the Soul in Western Philosophy and Science.*

THE LITURGY

Review of *The High Church Tradition* by G.W.O. Addleshaw; *Time and Tide*, 1941.

T his book is a study of the liturgy of the Church of England as it was received by the Anglican divines of the 17th century. "The superficial writer on religious matters would not gain a hearing in the 17th century, unless his superficialities had been purged away by a knowledge of the Fathers. Unless he had read his Chrysostom...his opinions would have been ruled out of court." These are healthy sentences for present-day writers to consider; those learned clergymen are no longer figures of fun. To dispute with them, as Johnson said of the poets of something the same period, "it was at least necessary to read and think." They, as it were, breathed orthodoxy; therefore the liturgy was their natural and holy speech. Mr. Addleshaw quotes from one of them, Thomas Comber, a description of it as "the life and soul of religion, the *anima mundi*, that universal soul which quickens, unites, and moves the whole Christian world."

It was not therefore their habit to twiddle and twist the *anima mundi* to the supposed momentary needs of the crowd— or indeed the Court. Edification and order were its secrets; the sacred City could not be built by everyone raising his own little pile of bricks. Men were to be part of it, and so only it of them. The eucharist, which was the center and consummation of all the rites, was the union of the City. "Sparrow...refers his readers to Saint Augustine's remark in the *De Civitate Dei* that the Christian sacrifice is the offering of the church as one body with its Lord."

The present difficulty is that we have lost the liturgical sense. There are, no doubt, excuses. The liturgy is almost bound to seem to us like one-half of a conversation in which the other speaker is entirely silent. We keep on saying things to God, and God says nothing. Entreaties, adorations, statements, are poured out; they cease; they begin again; but no other voice interrupts our own. We do what we can with lessons, psalms, gospels; we take, in an odd way, both sides, but then we have lost the natural sense of taking both sides; the priest's voice is no longer at times a reverberation of Another's. The sense therefore of a conversation *manqué* is over all.

It may be that this is to some extent at once the cause and the result of so many of our modern prayers and collects. I have sometimes wondered why, when the ecclesiastical authorities need something written, they so rarely turn to anyone whose business is writing. I am not offering myself as a candidate, though since it is to be supposed that a bishop administers his diocese better than I possibly could, there would be no particular egotism in supposing that I might be able to write better than a bishop. But the real trouble lies deeper than the problem of authors; it involves the recovery of adoration, with all its related ideas. The liturgy is much more a thing done than a thing said. Ceremonial is the encouragement of this. Mr. Addleshaw quotes Bishop Andrewes as saying that if our worship is inward only, "with our hearts and not our hats," something necessary is lacking. The things said are the accompaniments of something done. It is not our business to listen to the other Conversationalist (except as we always should); we do not go to church in order "to get good." The good will, of course, happen, because the good is always happening; it is its nature.

Mr. Addleshaw discusses the relation of the liturgy to the community, and shows what efforts were made to keep the liturgy both ordered and free. "It was"—to those theologians—"the prayer of humanity." It was even more, and more even than the *anima mundi;* it was the voice of Christ in the church. So, it had in its own especial way a place in the Holy Trinity itself. It was man in his place there. This is what the respectable ordered service of the Church of England was. People once objected to it for being respectable. Odd! They even objected to putting on their best clothes and saving silver for the offertory. Yet even that was part of the ceremonial, of the thing done, of the order and high sacrifice. Now we have no best clothes we must do without, and I hope the objectors are happy.

THE CHURCH LOOKS
FORWARD

Of the two great methods of spirituality that he called the Ways of the Affirmation and the Rejection of Images, Williams acknowledged that the ascetic Way of Rejection has held a more prominent place in Christian history. He thought the time was ripe, however, for developing the Affirmative Way, and in this essay, originally published in *St. Martin's Review* (July 1940) he draws out some of its implications for the practical life of the church.

In fact, of course, the church does not, in her full existence, even on earth, look forward. She looks centrally, she looks at that which is not to be defined in terms of place and time. It is either the nature of God at which she looks or the nature of things as known in God. It is *now* that the kingdom of heaven is fulfilled, generally and individually.

Even in less absolute terms, the church must not look forward too much. Her future is in the movement of the Holy Ghost and the resolution of our temporal knowledge into terms of Christ is the doing of the Holy Ghost. But though this is the nature of her life, she knows it in the mode of our more usual life. She does not, and under present conditions she cannot, fully realize that continuity of glory. There is therefore a double sense in which it may be said that the church does look forward: it may be said to correspond to the two great virtues of faith and hope—faith in the nature of God, hope in the nature of things in God. These virtues are not mere abstractions; they are the names of substantial life in its different preoccupations. They are even the names of the physical body in its proper reaction to actuality; perhaps they have been too confined to the invisible operations of the soul.

The church is to be distinguished from the world. But the physical bodies of her members relate her very intensely to the world. The union of the church and the world is material in the flesh. But the world, taken in this sense, is not the only element in the flesh; the flesh, even apart from matters of Redemption, is not wholly fallen. It has indeed been dragged down with the soul. But the soul is illuminated to know the principles of the unfallen flesh, and in the Redemption to recover them after the new method, to discover the substitution of a new kind of experience for an old. Whether we always recognize the experience for what it is is another matter; our business is to pursue it under authority. There are two main directions. The first is concerned particularly with the nature of things in God; the second with the nature of God. Neither, of course, can exist entirely without the other. It is not possible for the Christian to attend only to men and women (say) and not at all to God in himself. But neither is it possible for him to attend only to God in himself and not at all to men and women. The most remote hermit generally has to attend occasionally to his own meal, however frugal. The most overworked doctor has to say the Lord's Prayer with its clauses concerning God in himself.

We may find the intensity of both these great ways of the soul (and of the church) revivified. It is possible that there may come to exist a fresh impulse of ascetic life in the church; and by asceticism I do not mean hardships of the body only but of the mind and of the soul: the hardships and martyrdoms necessary to all those who are called to a life of separation (so far as possible) from all "creatures." Such outbreaks of austere vocations have occurred often in the history of the church. This is a matter which can only be recognized by souls capable of and called to that vocation. It is, certainly, the duty of every member of the church to examine himself or herself whether he or she is called to such an interior work. And it is also a duty to give the correct answer without any regret or dissatisfaction. It is a duty if the answer is "no" quite as much as if it is "yes." There is likely to be as much rejection of ourselves on the one way as on the other.

It was once suggested—and the suggestion was made neither profanely nor scandalously—that among all the orders of the Christian church there lacked one to our sacred Lord as "a gluttonous man and a wine-bibber." Considering that the very term Christian rose as a term of abuse and was then adopted, these other terms of abuse may not be without their own value and instruction for us. Food and wine are here the definite symbols of the "creature," more so as a divine Way than the locusts and wild honey of the Precursor. It is the following of our Lord in this knowledge of the creature which has been a part of the work of Christendom and may well be a greater part in the future. The doctrine of our Lord as God with its corollaries took centuries to work out. It is, certainly, now attacked. It is in dispute between Christendom and all that is not Christendom. But it is not in dispute within Christendom; all that has been finished with. The other doctrine of his manhood, with its corollaries, has still to be worked out and put into action.

Its corollaries have indeed arisen during the last century, even more clearly than ever before. More and more Christians have felt it their absolute religious duty to ensure, as far as possible, the existence of a just State. Mr. Middleton Murry has pointed out that, under present conditions, we only succeed in establishing anything like a just State under immediate pressure of war. Until that pressure exists we are content to leave a heavy proportion of our citizens in a state of direct or indirect despair; in a state, that is to say, in which, humanly speaking, any gospel, even the Christian, is bound to be incapable of reception. It is forbidden to the Christian to entertain despair: how much more to inflict it!

Despair is infectious; a State in which it is unconsciously permitted to exist is lost. We may, however, leave that particular prospect for others: it is sufficient to say that the duty there incumbent on us arises as much from our Lord's physical relation to men and women as from the order of his deity.

It is something of the same sense that lies at the beginning of another problem to which the members of the church will have to address themselves—the problem of marriage. Speaking generally, we have up to the present time insisted on the morals of marriage but we have not based them on any doctrine of love. We have rejected divorce but we have done so without any clear idea of the reason; and it is much to be feared that, in rejecting it, we have called in the help of all kinds of fallacies, inaccuracies, and even definite untruths. Natural life produces a vision of beauties, energies, and glories about which the comments of the officers of the supernatural life seem anxiously inadequate. When the same inadequate voices declare that the corollary of those strange benefits must be a lifelong fidelity, they must expect to be asked why. One answer is that it has been proved socially desirable, which seems doubtful and even unlikely. Another is that it is the will of God, which (if likely) is inexplicable. A labor of intellects is required.

The last sentence brings us to a point of looking forward on which a great deal depends in all the preoccupations of the church. Her missionary and her contemplative activities depend, it is agreed, on the Holy Ghost. The activities of the Holy Ghost depend on nothing but itself. But the success of the activities of the Holy Ghost (within the church) does depend on a something beside itself—it depends on the honesty of Christians. The honesty of Christians is a very desirable and also a very difficult thing. There can be few Christians alive who have not been aware, in themselves or in each other, of that great temptation—"to lie on the Lord's behalf." It has in the past done untold harm to the church, and it will again unless it can be overcome. It takes many shapes. It is apt to *pretend*—to pretend that intellectual arguments are valid when it should be clear that they are fallacious, that moral iniquity exists where there is no proof of it, and so on. An extremely distinguished dignitary of the church once printed the statement that the proportion of happiness to unhappiness in a man's life was as nine to one—an absolutely unjustified statement. (I do not say it was false: the whole point is that one ought not to make that sort of generalization at all; it is unprovable.) This kind of thing is still too common. Accuracy, accuracy, and again accuracy! accuracy of mind and accuracy of emotion. If the church is to look forward to a wholesome mental life her members must discipline themselves to honesty. The indulgence of any prejudice must be regarded as sinful, and an intellectual sin is as bad as a physical.

Yet the life of the church is single and not divided into intellectual and physical, and in her (militant here upon earth) the two affect each other as much as in any of her children. If her honesty can be recovered there might be recovered with it the fullness of her charismatic and prophetic ministry. It is not in any sense to deny the order which has developed in the church to say that the New Testament seems to contemplate the charismatic ministry as being the common possession of all believers. Whatever texts may be regarded as symbolic and whatever as literal, it is hardly possible to regard as other than literal the promise of a new life which shall be unharmed by earthly accidents, though not perhaps by earthly malignity. The disciples may be put out of the synagogues or even killed by the hatred (the righteous hatred) of those who conceive that they are doing God service so. But the casual "deadly things"—the serpent or the accidental venom—are to be harmless as far as they are concerned. And if those, then perhaps the accidental diseases and dangers of ordinary human life also—unless indeed those were, in certain cases, deliberately welcomed on behalf of others and in the cause and name of charity.

The rediscovery of such a high power as normal to the operative Christian is far enough away at present, and it is difficult to imagine how it might come. Nor indeed is it altogether desirable to imagine it coming; it is probably true that we shall never reach that state unless and until we are willing to welcome those distresses on behalf of others. We have lost, I think, to a very large extent the idea that we can effectively welcome them; it lingers chiefly in the intuitive natural desire of men and women at rare moments and under rare conditions. But conditions which are comparatively rare in the life of "the flesh" should be comparatively common in the life of "the spirit"—not meaning, by those words, the visible and invisible parts of our organism. What is necessary is the life of "faith," the substantial existence in us which we call faith. It is our business to recover that. The Holy Ghost will then do what he will, and it seems possible that we may humbly believe that at the right hour he shall teach us "what we shall speak"—when to make offers and when to receive offers, when to dismiss "devils" and when to endure them.

The doctrine of the Christian church depends on the substitution, in the last experiences, of our sacred Lord for us. The activity of the Christian church may have to recover, more than is commonly supposed, our substitution, one for another. The most important thing is to get our minds accustomed to the idea of that activity: attention without fever, speed without haste. The Atonement of our Lord restored this power to man; the Holy Ghost now, as originally, confirms, nourishes, and directs it. In the old legend Adam and Eve were, originally, one being. It is a profound symbol. Justice, charity, union; these are the three degrees of the Way of the Affirmation of Images, and all of us are to be the images affirmed.

THE ORDER OF THE
CO-INHERENCE

The first four paragraphs here, originally the final
section of *The Descent of the Dove*, sum up Williams's understanding of the dynamic solidarity he
called "co-inherence." He concludes with suggestions
as to the establishment of an order within the church,
for which he later composed the seven statements of
principle that follow.

t the beginning of life in the natural order is an act
of substitution and co-inherence. A man can have no
child unless his seed is received and carried by a
woman; a woman can have no child unless she receives and carries the seed of a man—literally bearing
the burden. It is not only a mutual act; it is a mutual act of
substitution. The child itself for nine months literally co-inheres in its mother; there is no human creature that has not
sprung from such a period of such an interior growth.

In that natural co-inherence the Christian church has understood another; the about-to-be-born already co-inheres in
an ancestral and contemporary guilt. It is shapen in wickedness, and in sin has its mother conceived it [Ps. 51:5]. The
fundamental fact of itself is already opposed to the principle

of the universe; it knows that good as evil, and therefore it derives and desires its own good disorderly. It has been sown in corruption, and in corruption it emerges into separate life.

It has been the habit of the church to baptize it, as soon as it has emerged, by the formula of the Trinity-in-Unity. As it passes from the most material co-inherence it is received into the supernatural; and it is received by a deliberate act. The godparents present themselves as its substitutes; by their intentions and their belief (and they are there to present even for "those of riper years") the newborn is granted "that which by nature he cannot have," he is "incorporated" into the church, he is made "partaker" of death and resurrection. It is this co-inherence which, at the confirmation, he himself confesses and ratifies.

The faith into which he is received has declared that principle to be the root and the pattern of the supernatural as of the natural world. And the faith is the only body to have done so. It has proclaimed that this is due to the deliberate choice and operation of the divine Word. Had he willed, he could presumably have raised for his Incarnation a body in some other way than he chose. But he preferred to shape himself within the womb, to become hereditary, to owe to humanity the flesh he divinitized by the same principle—"not by conversion of the Godhead into flesh, but by taking of the manhood into God." By an act of substitution he reconciled the natural world with the world of the kingdom of heaven, sensuality with substance. He restored substitution and co-inherence everywhere; up and down the ladder of that great substitution all our lesser substitutions run; within that sublime co-inherence all our lesser co-inherences inhere. And when the Christian church desired to define the nature of the Alone, she found no other term; It mutually co-inheres by Its own nature. The triune formula by which the child is baptized is precisely the incomprehensible formula of this.

It is supernatural, but also it is natural. The dreams of nationality and communism use no other language. The denunciation of individualism means this or it means nothing. The praise of individualism must allow for this or it is mere impossible anarchy. It is experienced, at their best moments of delight, by lovers and friends. It is the manner of childbirth. It is the image everywhere of supernatural charity, and the measure of this or of the refusal of this is the cause of all the images. The apprehension of this order, in nature and in grace, without and within Christendom, should be, now, one of our chief concerns; it might indeed be worth the foundation of an order within the Christian church. Such a foundation would, in one sense, mean nothing, for all that it could do is already exposed and prepared, and the church has suffered something from its interior organizations. About this there need be little organization; it could do no more than communicate an increased awareness of that duty which is part of the very nature of the church itself. But in our present distresses, of international and social schism, among the praises of separation here or there, the pattern might be stressed, the image affirmed. The Order of the Co-inherence would exist only for that, to meditate and practice it. The principle is one of the open secrets of the saints; we might draw the smallest step nearer sanctity if we used it. Substitutions in love, exchanges in love, are a part of it; "oneself" and "others" are only the specialized terms of its technique. The technique needs much discovery; the order would have no easy labor. But, more than can be imagined, it might find that, in this present world, its labor was never more needed, its concentration never more important, its profit never perhaps more great.

Williams drew up this list for the Order of the Co-in-herence some time in 1939. The copies that exist have minor variations.

1   The Order has no constitution except in its members. As it was said: *Others he saved, himself he cannot save.*

2   It recommends nevertheless that its members shall make a formal act of union with it and of recognition of their own nature. As it was said: *Am I my brother's keeper?*

3   Its concern is the practice of the apprehension of the Co-inherence both as a natural and a supernatural principle. As it was said: *Let us make man in Our image.*

4   It is therefore, *per necessitatem*, Christian. As it was said: *And whoever says there was when this was not, let him be anathema.*[1]

5   It recommends therefore the study, on the contemplative side, of the Co-inherence of the Holy and Blessed Trinity, of the Two Natures in the Single Person, of the Mother and Son, of the communicated Eucharist, and of the whole Catholic Church. As it was said: *figlia del tuo figlio.*[2] And, on the active side, of methods of exchange, in the State, in all forms of love, and in all natural things, such as childbirth. As it was said: *Bear ye one another's burdens.*

6   It includes in the Divine Substitution of Messias all forms of exchange and substitution, and it invokes this Act as the root of all. As it was said: *We must become, as it were, a double man.*[3]

7   The Order will associate itself primarily with four feasts: the Feast of the Annunciation, the Feast of the

Blessed Trinity, the Feast of the Transfiguration, and
the Commemoration of All Souls. As it was said: *Another will be in me and I in him.*[4]

Endnotes

1. A condemnation of Arianism attached to the creed promulgated in 325
at the council of Nicea. "There was when he was not," as it is usually translated, was an Arian slogan referring to the Word as inferior and subsequent to the Father. [C.H.]

2. "Daughter of thy Son," used by Dante in reference to the Virgin Mary.
[C.H.]

3. For the passage from which Williams adapted this line, see "The Way of
Exchange" below. [C.H.]

4. While she was in prison awaiting her martyrdom in 203, Saint Felicitas
bore a child. When she screamed the jailer asked how she expected to endure the greater pain in store. "Then," she answered, "another will be in
me who will suffer for me, as I shall suffer for him." Williams tells the story
in the second chapter of *The Descent of the Dove*. [C.H.]

THE REDEEMED CITY

As an image of co-inherence, the City holds a central place in Williams's thought. This essay, published in the *Dublin Review* (October 1941), brings it to bear on a theological interpretation of the reasons for which the second World War was being fought. Borrowing from Voltaire, he contrasts "the Infamy" and its habitual exclusiveness with the vicarious mutuality that constitutes the City. Between the two, the choice finally lies between a willingness and an unwillingness to forgive.

The differences between us and our enemy are many, and there are many different ways of summing them up. One of the more useful is perhaps that implied in the difference between the Race and the City. Whether the doctrine of Race be true need not much concern Christians; since they are not allowed to accept it as a definition of the final state of man, it can be, like any other scientific question, but a matter of minor if notable interest. There is no final idea for us but the glory of God in the redeemed and universal union—call it man or the church or the City. It is true that in the present crisis we are not disabled from gratefully accepting the aid of those great allies who, on human grounds, accept the same idea of the City in a more limited sense. The noble republicans of earth, the great humanitarian champions, are to be welcomed with respect and admiration. The lack in their vision of union is that they cannot include the dead; the past, for them, is indeed past, and its agonies remain for ever unatoned. But they have done much, and we owe them all but that which God alone could do. The words of Burke to Wilberforce can be used to them: "the House, the nation, and Europe," he said, "are under great and serious obligations to the honourable gentleman"— on that May night when the motion against the slave trade was put forward. Wilberforce was a Christian, but Voltaire was no Christian, and Saint Francis was a more orthodox Christian; and yet all of them were striking at one evil, at "the grand Infamy"—the horror of human tyranny, cold and cruel. That Infamy has been found both within and without the church; it is always the enemy of the church, and betrays it where it does not deny.

It is not, however, those noble allies with whom we are now directly concerned. It is our advantage—wholly undeserved—that their heroism is not incompatible with our belief, though they may suppose (largely because of the operation of the Infamy in the past) that our beliefs are incompatible with their desires. The Infamy is one and the same everywhere. The opposite of the Infamy is the City. There is, in the end, no compromise between the two; there is only choice. The choice exists everywhere, at every minute, as a fundamental, though that fundamental may have been accepted, and our business be with the edification of the City upon it. The thing in common between us and our allies, and in dispute between us and our enemies, is the proper freedom of the flesh. No one can, in fact, prevent a man thinking, or interfere with the motions the soul has in itself; what he can do is to prevent utterance. He can prevent the tongue speaking or the ears hearing; the other may or may not follow. All these things are worked out in terms of flesh, and must be; our Lord himself deigned to work out the conclusion of the whole matter in terms of flesh. It is the outrage upon the physical image of Christ, the physical vehicle of the Holy Ghost, which is the final impiety here. About the rest we cannot properly judge. The concentration camps and the tortures are the Infamy; the free talk and the nourishment of all bodies *(all* bodies) are the City. There is, in the end, no compromise.

The Holy Ghost moves us to be, by every means to which we are called, the images of Christ, the types of that Original, in or out of the flesh. It is the intercourse of those free images which is the union of the City. The name of the City is Union; the operation of the Infamy is by outrage on that union. The process of that union is by the method of free exchange. The methods of that exchange range from childbirth to the eucharist—the two primal activities of the earth and the church. There is, in the first case, a mutual willingness between the father and mother which results in the transference of seed. That it is so common does not lessen the trust implied; that one should abandon his seed to another, that one should receive the seed of another, is an exhibition of trust; it is almost the chief natural exhibition of that supernatural quality known as "faith"—a quality which has one of its own proper exhibitions in the interchange of the eucharist—"to effect the mystery of unity, we ourselves receive of that which is his what he himself received of that which is ours." So the Fourth Council of Lateran, decreeing in the highest things of earth the same doctrine of exchange; but decreeing them also through—I will not say the lowest, for the implication would be, as it has too often been, to reduce the flesh to an abasement unworthy of it. It was, no doubt, we who sinned, and sin, in the flesh; but the flesh itself retains for us many signs of that high calling from which we apostatized. Death itself is an outrage, a necessary outrage, upon a unity. We must accept it, as we must accept, for ourselves or for others, many another outrage. But it has been regarded, from the beginning, as an unnatural thing, a separation in the unseparated.

> *Within my soul there doth conduce a fight*
> *Of this strange nature, that a thing inseparate*
> *Divides more wider than the sky and earth.*

There is, there, no more rule "in unity itself."

Except by the restoration of the union. The high doctrine of the physical resurrection restores to mankind the unity of which it had been deprived. The new union can hardly be scarless; the original Unity, so again unified, must bear the marks of its wounds—as indeed it does: say, to name but one, of the spear-thrust in the side. Yet it is said that this, and the others, are "glorified." They wear a double radiance—of the original and of the renovation.

The Holy Ghost, it is declared, drives us towards a union with that Union. What he created, we must choose—accepting in the re-creation the original creation. That re-creation was presented to us, in the Apocalypse, under the image of a City. It is precisely the nations, and the races, who are to enter into it. The feast of Christ the King is also the feast of Christ the City. The principle of that City, and the gates of it, are the nature of Christ as the Holy Ghost exhibits it and inducts us into it; it is the doctrine that no man lives to himself or indeed *from* himself. This is the doctrine common to nature and grace.

There is, in those great myths which stand at the beginning of the Bible and hide from us and reveal to us the prolonged catastrophe of our fallen nature, the tale of the first murder. There is in it a very high symbolism. Cain and Abel both made offerings to the Lord. The divine Glory accepted Abel's and refused Cain's. There are all possibilities of interpretation, but among them is one which suggests that the very purpose of Cain's offering should have been that his brother's should be accepted; that it was in his refusal of this conclusion that Cain sinned. The fire from heaven fell, as is so often its habit, elsewhere than it was implored. The good descended—immediately, in answer to the prayer, as it had been asked, but not where it had been asked. The anger of the one who prayed and offered was aroused by this first of the substitutions; he slew his brother who profited. "Others have labored," said our Lord, laying down the same principle, "and ye have entered into their labors." He laid down that principle; he charged the apostles with the knowledge, and sent them to propagate it: this was to be the regeneration of earth, or at least an element in it. He did more; he declared it as his own. When, after his own substitution of himself for man, he talked with the disciples at Emmaus, he accused them of blindness to it: "O fools and slow of heart to believe all that the prophets have spoken, *ought* not Christ to have suffered these things and to enter into his glory?" And afterwards he celebrated for them the great exchange of the eucharist, and vanished. "Did not our hearts burn within us by the way?"

It was by an act of substitution that he renewed the City; this he had commanded as the order in both nature and grace. This is (to borrow Gerard Hopkins's word) the "inscape" of our hearts, and if the Infamy (in us and in others) has ruined that inscape by outrage, as war ruins landscapes and cities, still this is the inscape of the divine City. It is elementary enough, in our simple natural lives—from childbirth everyone who is not "a god or a beast" lives by that; there is no other way to live. We are, simply, utterly dependent on others, and it may seem that to stress it so much is to make us over conscious of a natural inevitability, to make our very breathing unctuous with a revolting piety. So perhaps it would be, if it were not for two things: (1) the universal nature of the application, (2) the supernatural nature of the principle. These two things, especially the first, the Infamy always denies.

It denies the first, precisely because it contradicts the City. Our Lord expressly reserved to himself any exclusion from the City. It is certain that he intimated, in the clearest words, the possibility of exclusion from the City; he called that exclusion hell. But he forbade his judgment to be forestalled; if his priests "retain" sins they do but remit them to himself. The nearest to adverse judgment that we can go is to pass on to his own judgment; the only judgment we are allowed to pronounce is pardon. Even that is only pronounced in his name; it is not for us to pardon from ourselves. But of that something more may be said presently.

The Infamy then denies inclusion. It denies it first by definition; that is, it makes definition an implicit and immediate exclusion from its own limits. Definition, of course, is necessary. To say "he is a German" or "she is a Christian" means that, and only that. It means the absence of certain characteristics and the presence of other characteristics. It may imply human arrangements. But it must not imply outrage. It must not, that is, exclude from the exchanges of nature, or indeed (in whatever sense) from the exchanges of super-nature. All it can do is to order those exchanges in one particular way instead of another particular way. It can make, as it were, "traffic regulations" for the convenience of traffic among men. It can clear our heads but it was never meant to petrify our hearts. Having defined, the Infamy proceeds to exclude, and then, so far as it can, to enslave or to annihilate. It may be observed at work in ourselves every day anywhere; for it is that which rejects in us a universal humility, a courtesy of carriage towards facts other than ourselves, a recognition of the creation even when that creation appears to us displeasing. It hides in the Christian church as much—or almost as much—as anywhere; the great image of it in literature is in the vision of the apostasy of the church at the end of Dante's *Purgatory*.

But (2) it denies the supernatural existence of the principle. This, indeed, as has been said, need not of itself be infamous; the republicans of earth may deny it, in denying the supernatural altogether. But it has frequently happened that they have denied the supernatural almost on behalf of its own republican principle; or, if not, then because of what they, with some justification, considered a lack of evidence. The Infamy denies it as part of its habit of exclusion. The evidence for this is again not only in our enemies today; it is in our hearts at all times. Against this denial the habit of the church in the baptismal rite has always testified. The newborn child emerges from its natural co-inherence in its mother into a supernatural co-inherence with the saints. It has received the communication of the evil of a fallen world; its blood is tainted from its soul—or from a world of souls—with the Infamy, and it will soon begin disastrously to pay back what it has disastrously received, in the exchanges (unless redeemed) of infernal conflict. At that moment it is caught by others and lifted into an exchange of grace—into others by others, into Another by Another.

As the practice of infant baptism became general in the church, this co-inherence was the more accentuated. The adult might speak for himself; the infant could speak only by others. Repentance and faith, the two first-felt and first-pledged qualities of the new life, had to be on its behalf felt and pledged by others. The inarticulate young creature, as it were, repented before he could sin and believed before he could think. Mystically vicarious, the sponsors were pledged; and their pledge was not released until, duly instructed in the vicarious life of the City, the subject of those pledges himself affirmed his own part in that life, and was permitted himself to approach the vicarious sacrifice and to feed on the vicarious nourishment. The operation of the Spirit, who is the life of the human image towards its divine original and had been so invoked in the baptism, claimed its votary in the confirmation. That life stretched before him, no more its own than it had been before, but now consciously known not to be its own.

To say so is not in any sense to deny its own responsibility. "Keep thy conscience with thy brother," said a hermit of the desert, "and thou shalt find rest." It is the individual conscience that must be kept so. The commandment to "bear one another's burdens" is full of great and sacred meanings, but it is, of course, still the individual who must bear; who must choose to bear and have courage to bear, no less than he must choose to relinquish and have courage to relinquish. "I am no companion for myself," wrote John Donne, "I must not be alone with myself....I am the Babylon that I must go out of, or I perish." The going-out is (to repeat a phrase) into the "inscape" of the heart, but that inscape can only be faithfully discovered by acts. He from whom the command to carry one another's burdens came promised that the burden should be light, but whether it is light or heavy can only be discovered by carrying it.

Nature compels and faith demands such a carrying; to quote Donne again: "the lights of nature and faith are subordinate John Baptists to Christ"; they are categories of one identity, the principle of the City, the formula of prophecy. It was uttered as a mockery by the incredulous when they saw the City in its agony; they said: "Others he saved; himself he could not save." It was irony, but the gospel is beyond irony; its affirmations are so literal that they are bound to seem ironical to the foolish, and the ironies of the foolish are discovered to be its own most precise definitions. He who could not save himself saved others, and required that we should be one with him in that, as in all. It may be added that he also reserved to himself the consciousness of that salvation; demanding perfection from us, he exactly forbade us the consciousness of perfection, even if it were achieved. "When ye have done *all,* say, we are unprofitable servants." The Glory is always to be observed in others; "ye are entered into *their* labors."

The unexclusive life of the City, then, is everywhere vicarious life, up to the level of each capacity. It is as much the instinct of a gentleman as the climax of the saints. The "bear one another's burdens" runs through all. The Infamy itself will use this, for its own profit, within itself, for the enslavement or destruction of others, as long as it is permitted to last; say, as long as its kingdom stands. Since it is impossible to escape this life, all that remains to us is to deepen it. In this sense to consider how we live *from* others may be even more profitable at times than to consider how we should live *for* others. Both are necessary to the perfect exchange. The methods of exchange, of carrying burdens and of giving up burdens to be carried; of acting in the strength of others; of making commitments by others; all these may be found to be full of meaning much beyond our ordinary understanding. It is the principle of the priesthood after its kind, and the principle of marriage after its kind.

It may be said perhaps of marriage with peculiar propriety that its lights of nature and faith are subordinate John Baptists to bring us to Christ the City. It is affirmed that marriage was instituted in the time of man's innocence, before the City was flawed or the perfect Body wounded. The fidelity which the church has declared to exist in marriage between Christians, and the finality in it which may be denied but cannot, this side of death, be destroyed, is of this nature, because there the nature of exchange has been accepted both in nature and in grace. The canonical conditions of marriage are rigorous for this reason; it is not proper that there should be any possibility of error. Accepted, they remain rigorous—an example of the truth that the vicarious and exchanged life which the divine Spirit commands and communicates is not less but more inexorable than the individual and single, and that that also has its hierarchy and order of behavior. In that life, as it moves in this life, the two shall be one; and the power which either draws on shall be double. This power may be for others besides them, but between them the opportunities of exchange are all to be thrown open. In this degree each may say, when the great experiment is done: "Myself I could not save; another I saved and another saved me."

Most clearly perhaps in marriage, but no less definitely in all relationships, the law of bearing one another's burdens exists. It exists necessarily as the active principle of life, and voluntarily as a duty only because our return to all active principles has to be treated as a duty. It is, in that great interior world, as if we had, in the exterior world, to be taught how to breathe. The air of goodwill is to be as universal as the actual air; presently we may fortunately be allowed to forget that we are breathing it. Meanwhile there remains to press, as far and as often as we can, in everyday affairs, the principle of vicarious life. The many common exchanges and substitutions of daily existence; the social balance of specialized occupations; the deaths and labors on behalf of others, and the deliberate acceptance of them, which are becoming more and more a part of our life at war; the inter-knit resistance to the enemy; the vigils of holy souls for others; the mystical substitution of the saints; the whole life of prayer and other experience which characterizes the church; the mystery of the Atonement; the veiled mystery of the Mother and the Son—*figlia del tuo figlio*—which is in some sense the center of the universe; and beyond the universe the co-inherence of the blessed and glorious Trinity itself—these are the expositions of the same identity.

Reposing in that identity, we may become conscious of it everywhere. More, much more, might be done by the practice of it between ourselves by intellectual and spiritual methods. Mental burdens can be carried as well as physical; and even physical more than we know. The very healing of the flesh might be hastened by it. It is not the reward of sanctity; it is a way of sanctity, but also it is the only way of bearable life. There again, of course, it is improper to be greedy or presumptuous: "in quietness and confidence shall be your strength." "Your life and your death," said Saint Anthony, "are with your neighbor." "And who is my neighbor?" The answer has been told us; the only alternative to that answer is to exclude something or someone from neighborhood. "I am to love myself," wrote William Law, "as I love my neighbour or any other created being, that is, only in and for God."

But, however apt we may be to this new life, it is certain we shall not escape committing or suffering outrage. The Infamy is too much with us for that. This commonality of evil leads to what is perhaps the deepest understanding of exchange, the exchange of pardon. Pardon in its proper nature is not a single but a mutual thing. There can be few relationships of any depth in which there is not some outrage to forgive; there are perhaps some few. Those who had to do with the saints can have had little to forgive, though the saints probably thought they had; it is what made them saints. To retain or remit a grudge is the choice between the Infamy and the City; it is the choice between the willingness to exclude another and the willingness to include another. Pardon as a disposition of the soul is a necessity—so long as the soul does not make too much of the business of forgiving. Even our Lord did not, when the outrage was worked on him, seem to forgive of himself: he referred it to his Father. Forgiveness is always, to the one who forgives, a grave spiritual danger. It should always *have happened.* Examples from literature are Imogen in *Cymbeline* and Miss Bates in *Emma;* both Shakespeare and Jane Austen knew sanctity.

Forgiveness then, with every kind of shyness, is a disposition, but to emerge as a perfect act it again needs an act and a mutual act. The two persons concerned must co-inhere in that mutual act, and pardon must be doubly welcome. Like joy (of which, at its best, it is a manifestation) it does not demand forgetfulness but acute knowledge. In our present state it may be wise sometimes to forget; the weight of our memories is too intense a weight of glory for us to bear. But that is an accident of our weak and temporal minds; in eternity it could not be so. "Every sin," said the Lady Julian of Norwich, "shall have worship in heaven"; and if this is to be so between the City and its inhabitants, then surely it must be so between the inhabitants themselves. So high a dream cannot be discussed here; only it may be said that this too is a state of exchange and of vicarious life. The offender lives the more intensely in the other's love. But to know it as love he must know it willingly; therefore he must desire it and ask it:

> ... *the circumference and form for ever*
> *In Forgiveness of Sins which is Self Annihilation;*
> *it is the Covenant of Jehovah.*

Such was Blake's definition of the "Perpetual Mutual Sacrifice in Great Eternity." The Infamy itself must be welcomed so; but if the Infamy knew it, it would already be one with the City. That is far beyond this discussion. But it may very well be a description of the Judgment which will discover how far we have seriously lived the vicarious life. "Wherein I find you," says an apocryphal record, "there will I judge you."

In the last paragraph of the Apostles' Creed the City is defined. "I believe in the Holy Ghost" is its first clause and primal condition. If it is living, it lives so, and only so, towards Christ; in whom it already lives complete, having (by virtue of his substitution) "the perfect and simultaneous possession of everlasting life."[1] Simultaneously all its citizens derive from all. "The Holy Catholic Church" is its name here, allowing for all proper implications of whatever kind: "visible—invisible," "invincible ignorance," and so on. But the other four clauses are, as it were, the four walls of the description in the Apocalypse; or, if the metaphor divides them too much, say they are the four qualities of that life: "the Communion of Saints, the Forgiveness of Sins, the Resurrection of the Body, and the Life everlasting." They are the qualities of the renewed perfection of union—interchange, interchange redeeming even the denial of itself, the glory of the holy flesh by which so much was known, the infinite power in all the glory. The glory is the thing happening; it is not, though in our talk we seem to make it so and can only believe in it so, an accident of the thing happening. The glory of God is in facts. The almost incredible nature of things is that there is no fact which is not in his glory. This is the great inclusion which makes the City. If, to use terms of space, we ascend towards it, it is still that which descends out of heaven, and is the cause and course of our ascent. The language of it is in the great interchange of fiery tongues by which the Spirit manifested at the beginning.

Endnotes

1. The definition of eternity that Thomas Aquinas borrowed from Boethius. [C.H.]

FORGIVENESS

The introductory chapter of *The Forgiveness of Sins,*
printed here with a new title and minus its final sentence, makes clear how important forgiveness was to
Williams as the deepest principle of the life of exchange and substitution, and gives an overview of the
approach he takes in the rest of the book.

How is it possible to write a book on the forgiveness
of sins? It is impossible. Great poets might do it, for
they understand everything; and saints, for they are
united with everything—creatures as well as Creator.
"I did pray all creatures," wrote Angela of Foligno,
"(seeing how that I had offended them inasmuch as I had offended the Creator), that they would not accuse me before
God. Then did it appear unto me that all creatures and all the
saints did have compassion upon me, wherefore with a
greater fire of love did I apply myself to praying unto God
more than was customary."

The principles of the universe are clear to both those
groups of sufferers. But other writers, who only repeat, more
or less intelligently, with more or less goodwill, what they
have been told; popularizers of the spirit whose duty is to the
next moment; pedants and propagandists and other plagia-
rists of man's heart—what do we know about it? what can we

say with any conviction, and with any style, of the crises of the spirit? We follow the fashion; the fashion, in our set, is to talk religion precisely as in other sets they talk films or finance. So we talk or we write; and, not having a high style to write in, not being able to manage words, we naturally persuade ourselves that colloquialisms and clichés are desirable. We must write for Everyman, and because it is reported that Everyman is crude, we must write crudely for him.

Yet if there is one thing which is obviously either a part of the universe or not—and on knowing whether it is or not our life depends—it is the forgiveness of sins. Our life depends on it in every sense. If there is God, if there is sin, if there is forgiveness, we must know it in order to live to him. If there are men, and if forgiveness is part of the interchanged life of men, then we must know it in order to live to and among them. Forgiveness, if it is at all a principle of that interchanged life, is certainly the deepest of all; if it is not, then the whole principle of interchange is false. If the principle of retributive justice is our only hope we had certainly better know it. Because then, since retributive justice strictly existing everywhere is staringly impossible, all our hopes of interchange and union, of all kinds, are ended at once; and we had better know *that.*

It is not, however, in this human discussion of the possibilities of forgiveness that the dark terror lies. We can happily universalize our individual experiences into theories there without feeling much horror, though not perhaps without doing some harm. The fear is in making statements about God. There both the possibility of truth and the possibility of communication fail. Neither rhetoric nor meiosis will serve; the kingdom of heaven will not be defined by inexact terms, and exact terms....Exact terms! It is not altogether surprising that we are driven back sometimes on irony, even on a certain bitterness. At least, so, we acknowledge the impossibility of the task; besides, we may find that our ironies are merely true. Irony is perhaps cheap but it is useful: it is (to use a metaphor itself ironic, cheap, and useful) a gas-mask against heaven. It is true we shall find we are carefully wearing it against pure air—that is the irony. But we should not at first have been able to bear the pure air without protection—that is the truth. It was the laughter of Beatrice in heaven which had once to be spared Dante—her laughter and heaven's song. The false smile of irony spares us for a while from the true smile of heaven.

All then that can really be hoped is that some semi-attentive reader, distrusting or despising what he reads, may turn from it to consider in himself the nature of forgiveness; so, and only so, can this consideration hope to be of any use. It is, as our Lord told us long ago, only the compulsion of the soul that leads to a true knowledge of the doctrine. It is true the comprehension of the blood beats with the same knowledge, though there not understood. Discussion and speculation are amusing enough; there are twenty-four hours in every day and they have to be got through somehow. Any fool can invent theories of the Fall, and when fools were interested in theology they frequently did; nowadays they are more concerned with economics or strategy or "ideals." Any fool can discuss how or what God, from his pure self-existence, knows, creates, or sustains. Even in reading the great doctors we sometimes become conscious of a sudden revolt, not perhaps in itself unwise. "The holy intellect," "our blessed reason"—we are like Wordsworth; we are bound to

> deem our blessed reason of least use
> Where wanted most.

The application of the finite to the infinite must surely always be wrong? Since we can never have all the premises, how can our conclusions ever be true? Just; yet the blood holds the need; our physical natures awake thought and even in some sense think; they measure good and evil after their kind. The easy talk of mental distress being worse than physical may occasionally be true; only occasionally. Most men would prefer a month's mental distress to a month's serious neuralgia. It is in our bodies that the secrets exist. Propitiation, expiation, forgiveness, are maintained *there* when the mind has explained them away—the need, and the means, and the fruition.

The secrets of extreme heaven and the secrets of extreme earth are both obscure to us. It is between these realities that explanation and diagram inadequately lie. The ways of approach are two. One may begin by considering pardon as a fact in human life, and so proceed to a meditation on its nature as a divine act. Or one may begin by considering it as a divine act and so conclude with the human. Discussions of human experience are nearly always unsatisfactory. To ask "do we not all know?" or "have we not all felt?" by the mere phrasing of the sentence convinces the reader that he has neither known nor felt. But some idea of pardon as men have known it is necessary as a description if not as a definition.

THE TECHNIQUE of PARDON

The four chapters of *The Forgiveness of Sins* that precede this one discuss forgiveness in Shakespeare, the "chosen catastrophe" of the Fall, and forgiveness in the Old and New Testaments. Here Williams turns to practical applications, personal and political. The first sentence, which originally made reference to the previous chapter, has been altered.

There are three chief modes in which we understand forgiveness in its own high and lofty style. The virtues, owing to the laborious detail in which they have to be pursued by us (and we can only pursue them in laborious detail—"general good," said Blake, "is the plea of the scoundrel, hypocrite, and flatterer")—the virtues are apt to be subdued to our own niggling style. But in themselves they are not so; they are gay and princely; and so they are seen when they are recognized in others simply because we are in a state of love towards others.

We can admire them in their freedom in others when in ourselves they must seem, if not in servitude, at least only just escaped from servitude, sore from the manacles, bleeding from their effort at freedom, lame, purblind, unheavenly. It is our business to admire them heavenly whenever they can be so seen; the opportunity is in such states as marriage and friendship, and we do very well to take it whenever it is found. "This ought ye to have done, and not to have left the other undone." We must not cease from our own labor because the glory is seen free in another; but neither must we cease to admire the glory because the labor is all that we can feel in ourselves. Nevertheless we might unconsciously learn to carry even grace with an air; it is not ours, and so we may; we have nothing to be proud of; another has labored and we are entered into his labor. An unconscious magnificence of any virtue is only to be attained by the practice of that virtue combined with humility. Since this is bound to be conscious, it is not always easy to achieve its opposite; but in itself the grace of "the weight of glory" is precisely its lightness.

It may be suggested therefore that forgiveness can be considered as applicable in three ways: (1) to things which need not be forgiven; (2) to things which can be forgiven; (3) to things which cannot be forgiven. The first and the third, put so, are contradictory; nevertheless, the phrases may for the present stand.

(1) Things which need not be forgiven. There is a tendency among some Christians to make a burden of things which non-Christians would pass over lightly. They overdo forgiveness as they overdo patience and other virtues. No doubt Christianity and life ought to be one; no doubt, essentially, they *are* one; that is why we are at odds with both, because we are still often at odds with that which is the root of both. No doubt we ought to be always looking for opportunities of leading the Christian life. But there are two ways of doing even that—one is with courtesy and the other without courtesy.

Courtesy is our whole business towards our neighbors; it is indeed spiritual self-preservation; well, but then so is love. Love, we have been told, is slow to anger; it is, as a result, slow to forgive, for it will not be in a hurry to assume that there is anything to forgive; and if there is, it will not be in a hurry to make a business of forgiving. Many lives are passed without the experience of anything in others which can seriously be supposed to need forgiveness, though not indeed without themselves committing wrongs which may seem to need forgiveness. I do not mean here only that we should not make an exterior fuss; we should not even make an interior fuss. The good manners of the City of God are supernaturally instinctive; the instinct of the new life should warn us of any approaching danger of pomposity or guile, and the danger is subtle. The new way—forgiveness, humility, clarity, charity—is there; it is the old man on the new way who is the tempter, and who beguiles us away from it while we think we are walking on it. We cannot, and need not, when we seem to be insulted or injured, be unaware of it; but we can dismiss the awareness with a shrug or a smile—at ourselves. "A sense of humor" has been overpraised; wit would be better, could we attain it, but it must be a whole and healthy wit, and it should be but an instrument at first. Love "doth not behave itself unseemly"; that is, it carries itself beautifully; it takes no need to itself. An awareness of injury, unless it has been deeply aimed at the heart, is exactly taking heed to oneself; an awareness of forgiveness, unless it is asked, is apt to be a taking heed to itself. Not to be quick to forgive in this sense is as much a part of the divine command as not to be slow is in another; we have to be free; even from the virtues, in the end.

(2) Things which can be forgiven. But how then to distinguish, to carry ourselves handsomely, to avoid rejoicing in iniquity? Rejoicing in other people's iniquity, one way or another, is a not uncommon fault. There is at least one simple distinction, even if it cannot always be used; it lies in the request for forgiveness. Saint Peter, in the dialogue with Emmanuel mentioned earlier [Matt. 18:21-22], included this as a condition, and our Lord permitted it: "if my brother sin

against me and turn again?" The question here is of serious, but not fatal, harm; injuries which wound but do not kill the heart; blows which might be returned in anger but not with a cold and determined vengeance; such wounds as leave love, where it is felt, still felt as in being. We may be permitted perhaps to take the term "my brother" as significant there; at least, for the present purpose. Say, that the consciousness of brotherhood, of relationship, is still vital; it is within that relationship that the harm has been done. It is then within that relationship that the forgiveness must exist, and since all relationship must thrive or decay by what it holds within it, by its elements, it is from such forgiveness that the relationship must thrive. But then, since mutual love thrives from mutual acts, the forgiveness must be a mutual act, an act of agreement. Love, indeed, in that sense, is mutuality; the effort to practice love is an effort to become mutual; that is where it goes beyond what is generally called "unselfishness." To prefer another's will to one's own is much, but to become another's will by means of one's own is more, and is indeed the necessary thing for love.

"Love," said Saint Thomas, "is nothing else than the willing of good" to the beloved; and when the functions of the beloved are exercised in the good, there one must love the beloved in his or her functions; one must will those functions, and be a power towards them. The union of lovers is in that double energy. It is true indeed that he is unwise who falls into the pseudo-romantic illusion of saying: "O I can only do it *if* ..."; who demands companionship before he can be industrious and love before he can be chaste. "They only can do it with you who can do it without you." But, that being so, there can be an added power; as it were, the oxygen to the mountain-climber. No doubt, if one cylinder were not there, another would serve; there is nothing sacrosanct about oneself; anything might do as well. But if one is required to be oxygen, one had better be oxygen.

This where and as it applies. In some things it does not apply. Thus the most intense physical form of mutuality is, normally, in intercourse between the sexes; the most perfected, there, that which results in childbirth. But the physical form is but one, and not, for all the mystery of the body, in the end the most important. Many separated lovers have discovered that. Of the spiritual functions, the realization of a sense of sin is one, and of repentance, and of pardon. A double energy should go to it. This is not to say that it is the lover's business to impose a sense of sin on, or to demand it from, the beloved; he would be a fool who was thus rash; more especially he would be a fool who did so without a great and piercing sense of exchange. Guilt is in all; it is the guilty who forgives. Entreated to forgive, by another as guilty, it is his whole duty to restore reconciliation by any and every means, for ever and ever, without condition. The protested single guilt on the part of another leads more easily to a sense of one's own single guilt; therefore to a sharing of the condition of guilt.

The entreaty for forgiveness does not, among mortal creatures, abolish the sin, but it does a little transform it. It transforms it doubly; it provokes a shy humility on the part not only of the pardoned but of the pardoner. The awful consciousness (in any serious matter) that he is necessarily exercising, in his proper degree, the conceded prerogative of Christ, prevents pride, prevents anything but shame. Must the lecherous forgive the malicious? the slothful the arrogant? it seems no less. But not, surely, without a keener sense of lechery or sloth, a renewed entreaty on his own part, a confessed exchange of guilt. Not perhaps, vocally, then and there; it is sometimes a solecism to intrude one's own sins, though hardly to remember them secretly.

"The falling out of faithful friends renewing is of love"; the old poem has a deeper sense than perhaps it altogether meant. The word "faithful" certainly has. The mutual operation is an operation of "faith"; it is a further entering into "the substance of things hoped for," a further exhibition of "the evidence of things not seen." It may be objected that such operations, in many and many a relationship of love, are purely "natural"; they neither invoke, nor think of invoking, the supernatural world of which Saint Paul was thinking. So; but then the great goods do operate naturally. Where there is love, there is Christ; where there is human reconciliation, there is the church. To say so is not in any way to weaken the supernatural: where the consciousness of that exists, the power of the operation ought in every way to pierce deeper, to last longer, to live stronger, than in the natural. The invocation of Emmanuel is at the root of all, and where the invocation is conscious the consciousness of love should be greater. "Ought"…"should"…it is staringly obvious that in our present age it does not. The children of this world are even now in that other wiser than the children of light. And indeed for many of us it is the natural passion of love rather than the supernatural principle which directs and encourages us. This is well enough; it is more than well; so long as we intend to pursue the natural into the more-than-natural of which it is a part. The real distinction between Christians and non-Christians is here, as always, something very like the risk of hell. He who professes a supernatural validity for his virtuous acts must follow them out into that whole validity. He who professes only nature may be rewarded with the best of nature, perhaps with more than nature; he who professes more than nature, if he does not practice it, may be left with neither. "Unto him that hath shall be given; from him that hath not shall be taken away even that which he seemeth to have."

It is in relation to the next heading that the dependence of the natural on the supernatural can be again raised.

(3) Things which cannot be forgiven. The phrase is only humanly true, and (everything considered) it is perhaps not even that. It would be dangerous to say that there is any princely goodness of which the human spirit is not capable; its original derivation beats in it still, and its divine kinship moves still in brain and blood. A perfection of pardon is not only a Christian dream. But it is, if not only, yet certainly, a Christian doctrine. Whether a pagan ought to forgive all injuries may depend on his own knowledge of spirit, on his "inner light." But it depends on no such unsure thing in a Christian; it depends on the will of Christ and the doctrine of the church. The Christian has no doubt of his duty, though he may have every difficulty in fulfilling it. He is not, in that, very different from the faithful of other great religions; the Buddhist is a recipient of the same spiritual command. The difference between them, in that, is of another order. Forgiveness of all injuries is demanded of the Christian because of the nature of our Lord, and it is demanded entirely. The phrase "things that cannot be forgiven" is therefore to him intellectually meaningless.

But it may in fact mean a good deal all the same. It is true that few of us are, fortunately, in a position to understand that meaning; no injuries of which the forgiveness seems unbelievable have ever been done us. But probably there are at the present moment more persons alive in Europe than for many generations to whom such injuries have been done. The forgiveness of the poor—even if a casual and pagan pardon; say, rather, the lack of resentment in the poor—we have had always with us, little though we have cared to understand it. But the massacres, the tortures, and the slavery, which have appeared in Europe of late have impressed themselves upon us. In the ruined houses of Rotterdam—or indeed of England—among the oppressed thousands of Poland, there are those to whom the phrase "things that cannot be forgiven" has a fearful meaning. Must they nevertheless be forgiven? they must. Must vengeance, must even resentment, be put off? it must. There is certainly a distinction between the desire for private vengeance and the execution of public justice. But there is no excuse for concealing private vengeance under the disguise of public justice. The establishment of tribunals to impose penalties for breach of treaty-agreements is, I suppose, possible; how much more, if anything, may be either possible or desirable we need not here discuss. It would have nothing to do with its main theme; and indeed of that main theme Rotterdam and Poland are only contemporary and spectacular examples, chosen for convenience. The injury done to many in that kind of war is greater than the injury done to one in private, but the result, from a Christian point of view, cannot be other. That must be, everywhere and always, the renewal of love. But in such a state as we are now considering, that renewal of love means little less than heroic sanctity. It is upon such heroic sanctities that the church depends—depends in the sense that they are its rule, its energy, and its great examples. It is less likely, when the hurt is so deep, that there will be any request for forgiveness. The deeper the injury, the less inclined the evildoer is to ask, even to desire, that the sin may be forgiven—perhaps the less able. Remorse rather than repentance—with all that repentance means—is likely to exist; there is already present the possibility of that kind of half-anger, half-anguish which is too easily built up into a continued wickedness, a separate hell.

The depth of vengeance on one side; on the other, at best remorse, at worst persistence in injury—can these be turned into the reconciliation of love? It is at least in such states of all but everlasting conflict that the church expects the coming of peace, and that she demands, on the side of the injured, the heroic sanctity of pardon, or the interior preparation for it. In itself it may not properly exist until an opportunity is given it by the request; it cannot be mutual till then; therefore it cannot, in itself, *be* till then. But the whole passion of it must be there, waiting for the second's opportunity; the spirit waiting for the letter, without which it cannot perfectly be. And here again it is to be maintained that, even in such difficult moments, the double responsibility of guilt enters; sinner to sinner. Heroic sanctity is required perhaps to forgive, but not to forgive is ordinary sin. There is no alternative; the greatness of the injury cannot supply that. It becomes—an excuse? no, a temptation: the greater the injury, the greater the temptation; the more excusable the sin, the no less sin.

It was said at the beginning of this book that it was impossible to write such a book; and besides the impossibility of the theme, here is a side impossibility. Can any writer lay down such rules, for himself and for others—especially for others? No; and yet without those rules, without that appalling diagram of integrity, there can be no understanding, however small, of the nature of the interchange of love. For on the achievement in the extreme all depends. The courtesies of our first division, the intimacies of the second, spring only from the truth that the fact of forgiveness is absolute. Emmanuel, by his existence in flesh, by his victimization, by his life as forgiveness, and by his proclamation of forgiveness, showed it as absolute. In doctrine and in action, the church maintains the fact.

There are two footnotes, as it were, which should be added to the consideration of all three divisions. The first might be called the Rule of the Second Step. In matters of forgiveness, as in all other virtues (and some vices) the first step is comparatively simple compared to the second. Hell is always waiting for the rebound. The only prevention of the rebound is perseverance. The first moment of forgiveness is nearly always confused with other things—with affection, with delight, with honor, with pride, with love of power; some good, some bad, all distracting. It will happen, often enough, that the forgiveness is rather an emanation of these things than a power in itself. But then, directly afterwards, the good elements will withdraw themselves and leave the reconciliation to its own serious energy; and if that energy is too weak, it will break; but it will not break alone, for the affection and the joy will be hurt too. Or else the evil elements, the pride and the sense of power, will dominate the reconciliation, and it will become egotistical and a false illusion of the good. Even the light courtesies and settings-aside of our first division need sometimes a second shrug: nothing is achieved at once.

> *The horse is taught his manage, and no star*
> *Of wildest course but treads back his own steps;*
> *For the spent hurricane the air provides*
> *As fierce a successor; the tide retreats*
> *But to return out of its hiding-place*
> *In the great deep all things have second birth.*

The virtues, however wild their course, have to tread back their own steps; they have, young and innocent, to be taught their manage. They have to learn to be always ready when they are called on; so, they may in time, but only in time, be ready without the calling; their obedience to time and place in us sets them there outside those conditions in the end: "servitude and freedom are one and interchangeable."

It is in relation to this management that the second footnote may be useful: a footnote on recollection. There are two methods of reconciliation: that which remembers the injury in love and that which forgets the injury in love. It is a delicate technique of pardon which can distinguish and (without self-consciousness) use either. Either may be desirable here and now, though there can, of course, be no question which is finally desirable and even necessary to the existence of the Blessed City. There (its architect told us and all its architecture maintains) all things are to be known. We had better not forget it; but even so, "he that believeth shall not make haste." Oblivion—say, perfect seclusion of the injury in God—is often here a safer means. It is often likely that to remember the injury would lead only to some opposite injury. Even the best-intentioned Christians are not always at ease in these sublime states. The mutual act of forgiveness can, too often and too quickly, become a single memory of the sin; the single memory a monstrous interior repetition of recollection; the monstrosity a boredom; the boredom a burden. Or, worse, the sense of superiority is too easily involved. We may say and think we have forgiven and then find we have not; or, worse again, think we have forgiven, and in that self-deception *never* find that we have not; we may die supposing ourselves to be kindly and self-pleasingly and virtuously reconciled—"And then will I profess unto them, I never knew you; depart from me, ye that work iniquity." But also we may in fact have forgiven—say, half-forgiven; and the pardon is thought to free the pardoner to every claim and compel the pardoned to every obedience. "Such," wrote Blake,

> *Such is the Forgiveness of the Gods, the Moral Virtues of the*
> *Heathen, whose tender Mercies are Cruelty. But Jehovah's Salvation*
> *Is without Money and without Price, in the Continual Forgiveness of Sins,*
> *In the Perpetual Mutual Sacrifice in Great Eternity: for behold,*
> *There is none that liveth and sinneth not.*

If it is forbidden to us to demand as a condition of our forgiveness any promise that the offence shall not be repeated, if when he conceded to us the declaration of reconciled love, God retained that condition to himself alone, how much more is it forbidden us to make any other claims, to expect an extra kindness, to ask for an extra indulgence. And how all but impossible to avoid! Forgiving or forgiven, we can claim nothing, at the same time that we have, in God, a right to claim everything. Conceding the permission to promulgate, he conceded also the right to demand; in the church such things happen. In sacramental confession itself it is the priest who (conditions fulfilled) cannot refuse absolution. Nor we forgiveness; the sinner has all the advantages, as the just son of the prodigal's father felt. But, so admitting, we can slide into an evil mutuality: how easy to claim consideration in return; or if not to claim, at least to expect; or if not to expect, at least to feel we have a right to—somewhere, somehow, *some* right! Alas, none but what our injurer, of free choice, gives us. Otherwise, the mutuality itself becomes diseased; it grows corrupt with the dreadful stench of the old man on the new way. To forget the sin is the safer method.

Yet oblivion too has its dangers. The beauty of the joyous and mutual interchange is bound to dwindle a little if the occasion is put aside; that is, between lovers. And in those other more austere instances, where love exists not as a strong and conscious affection, but only as a deliberate act of the will—in Rotterdam and Poland, say even there, though the soul can live from the wound of the heart, yet it is perhaps less easy to learn to do so if the hurt is put aside. Our derivation, our nourishment, is both from our sorrows and from our joys; it is so obvious, and so harsh and lengthy, a business to find it there. Say, Forget; and add, But do not say Forget.

Love must carry itself beautifully; it must have style. It may seem absurd, in such high matters, to use so common a literary term, and yet there is hardly any word so useful. Style, in literature, is an individual thing. *Le style, c'est l'homme même*—style is the man himself, said the French maxim. Considering what men are, it need not be pressed too far. Yeats indeed declared that a poet's work was often the anti-type of his individual nature; he quoted Keats and Dante as examples. But in religion the problem hardly arises; in religion we are dealing with "the man himself" and there can be no separation. His style is his particular manner of courtesy; his lack of style is his lack of courtesy. It may be sedate or glorious, distant or intimate, firm or even flamboyant. Only, if it exists at all, and to the level at which it exists, it will not be insincere or partial. A purity of virtue will do much; it cannot, in any one case, do all. What is needed in every case, in every virtue, in every act of every virtue, is that all purities of intention should be precisely there. Pardon is perhaps the act in which all are most needed; it is apt to grow false if any are missing; it is quite certain not, then or thereafter, to have its proper joy. It gathers up within itself all the powers of love, because in fact it is love—chaste with the glowing chastity of the divine Son. Chastity is the spirit of which courtesy is the letter; the spirit waits for the letter and the letter for the spirit; both together are love—love in knowledge, which is the only kind of love with which the Christian church has, finally, any concern.

It would sound absurd to say that pardon itself has, on earth and between men and women, to be pardoned. Yet some kind of occasional meditation on this might not be unwise. "They feel most injured who have done the wrong"; and even if they repent and ask for forgiveness, they quite frequently begin to feel the forgiveness as an injury when they have it. It is not easy to be forgiven; certainly not to continue in the knowledge of being forgiven. Only the princeliest souls can bear it naturally for long; only the holiest supernaturally—

by which word is meant there not the pardon of God for man, but the pardon of man for man in the church. There will be something selfish in the pardon; that, at least, will be resented, if nothing more—improperly resented, no doubt, but then it is itself an impropriety. Our very forgiveness is an opportunity for us to be forgiven—by God, of course, but also, and with more tardiness, on our side and his, by our neighbor. We were both sinners, we were both guilty—yes, originally; but also we are both sinners and guilty in the very act of penitence and pardon. Let it rest; it is the very promise of life.

Such then is the relationship which is to be attempted among the redeemed; which is, by virtue of something else, to be achieved. The union of all citizens of the City is not to leave out any facts. Everything that has ever happened is to be a part of it, so far as men are strong enough to bear it; the holier the stronger. Everything that has ever happened is an act of love or an act against love. Acts of love unite the City; acts against love disunite. But of this disunity it is necessary that we should not be too quickly aware. The Lady Julian laid down a great maxim when she said: "here was I learned that I should see my own sin, and not other men's sins, but if it may be for comfort and help of mine even-Christians." The earthly courtesy which we discussed under the first of the three headings above is a heavenly courtesy also. It is opposed to courtesy in all its degrees that we should be too quick to cast out the mote.

At the same time not even the greatest courtesy is blind. Love itself, as we know from Love itself, is not blind. If the mote in our neighbor's eye leads him to murder another neighbor, we may presumably notice it. We are permitted to remark it when his mote leads him to take away our coat, though we are not then to insist on pulling it out; we are, on the contrary, to offer our cloak also. It has been said a hundred times that on those principles no organized State could exist. It is clear also that it is precisely on those principles that the church is intended to exist, and does indeed exist; at least it has no others.

The transfiguration of the earthly State into the heavenly City is a work of the Holy Ghost. The word *transfiguration* there is apt; it is a change of diagram. It does not involve, as the Manichaeans do vainly talk, a putting-off of the natural body, but it does involve that natural body itself becoming accustomed to a whole new set of laws—at first as commands, then as habits, last as instincts. It has often been pointed out that we use the word "law" ambiguously; that the "laws" of the Decalogue are not the same thing as the "laws" of movement. The alteration of the one into the other, individually and generally, is the work of the Holy Spirit in the church. It is an age-long work, and it has to be done individually—even the general work has to be done individually.

Efforts have been made—not too successfully—to set up a Christian republic, a kind of Christian anarchy, in which the secular State with its laws and penalties should not exist. It is not merely from the greed or tyranny of the higher ecclesiastics that the church has so often felt uneasy with even the most admirable State. The State, as it were, longs to stand still; but the church cannot stand still. Her very name is speed; her mind is set always on virtues so great, on modes of living so intense, that we cannot begin to imagine them. The most elementary images of them are repulsive to us—except at rare moments, and even then we are not sure. Can we order all our affairs by instincts we hardly begin to feel? to assert it and to deny it is alike dangerous. Must we, for example, consent that men, other men, shall be killed and maimed?

The answer to that is simple—we must. We may do it by ourselves inflicting death and torment on others (by bombs or however), or we may do it by abandoning others to death and torment (in concentration camps or wherever), but one way or the other we have to consent by our mere acts. To call the one war and the other peace does not help. This—whichever it is—is certainly, in part, the result of what we do. Is there any direction? Even to quote "Thou shalt not kill" does not finally help, for we have been taught that consciously to abandon men to death is, in fact, to kill. To hate is to kill; to kill is to kill; and to leave to be killed is to kill; yes, though (like the lawyer in the gospel) we do not know who our neighbor is. There are wars to which that does not apply; there are wars to which it does. Such is the dilemma in which we find ourselves; and then what happens to forgiveness?

I have taken the most extreme example; but the root dilemma is common enough. It is a dilemma in which any man existing in an organized State is continually involved. Capital punishment, the whole penal law, the instability of the poor, a hundred social evils, are all part of it. To disagree with this and that no more helps us—or very little more—than to agree. While we remain part of the State we are involved in its life. Disagreeing leaves us where we were; we might as well disagree with the Fall, as no doubt most of us do. We cannot, so far, escape the nature of man, the original and awful co-inherence of man with man in which we were created. Certainly we must follow whichever path our conscience, under the authority of the church, indicates; we must disagree with one and agree with one as we are instructed. But the moral burden is the same both ways.

What then are we to say, in this matter of forgiveness, about the State, if anything? especially, if such a thing can indeed exist, about the Christian State? Morally, of course, in the Christian State, where its members were all Christians, the matter would be simple in essence, though perhaps complex in operation. The courts would operate in a parallel order to the confessionals—only the confessions would be public. But that would certainly involve repentance on the part of the guilty. Whether in a profoundly Christian State it would be possible for the church to produce a guild of those who would vicariously bear the legal penalties on the part of the confessed criminals, even perhaps to the death penalty itself, if that were still imposed, is but a dream. Yet only by operations that once seemed no less of dreams has the church reached its own present self-consciousness—by devotions not dissimilar, powers not otherwise practiced. We do well to dream such things as long as our dreams are in accord with the great Christian vision. This is only another example of substitution, upon which our Lord created the original universe, and which he afterwards reintroduced in his own awful Person as the basis of his redeemed world. Pardon itself is an example of it; the injured bears the trouble of another's sin; he who is forgiven receives the freedom of another's love.

We shall have certainly to remake the State before such things can be; humanly speaking, we shall have almost to remake the church. But then we can never quite talk of the church "humanly speaking," and the State we shall have to remake anyhow if it is to last and succeed even naturally. The bounty of the spirit then would be its freedom: our poverty can only rise into that bounty by the practice of such freedom as is found in a speed of giving and taking forgiveness.

"The State's function," it has been said, "is inherently ambiguous, and in some ways resembles that of the Law in Saint Paul's theology."[1] In the matter of the secular law that ambiguity is mostly to be discerned in the inevitable use of penalties. Punishments, under the State, are either retributive or reformatory. But either way they have to be enforced; they are put into operation by the decision and force of the magistrates very much against the will of the guilty. It is at least a question whether this, though our only method, is not from the fundamental Christian point of view a false method. The chief use of punishment in the State is to frighten the majority of citizens from behaving as they wish to behave, and as a minority do behave. But penance in the church is not of this nature, nor is it retributive nor reformatory. It is much more in the nature of something undertaken, as a "satisfaction," by the guilty and repentant person; it is, that is to say, *desired.* The idea of that state which is called "purgatory" is not different. That certainly is purging, is reformatory; but it is not entirely without the notion of compensation. The mountain of purgatory, wrote Dante, "shakes when some soul feels herself cleansed, and free to rise and mount....Of that cleansing the will makes proof, which seizing the soul with surprise avails it to fly. It wills indeed earlier, but is not then free from that desire which the divine justice, against the will, sets as once towards sin, so now to the torment." The will to reach God is counteracted by the desire for the compensation of sin. But this is in the pardoned souls; they are pardoned before they are in purgatory; it is why they are in purgatory.

This flame towards both pardon and punishment is the mark then of the elect soul. It has its parallels in lower spheres. Lent, it has been said, is no such unjoyous season; many a mortal lover, guilty of some offence, sighs for a penalty; Shakespeare, as we saw, sealed it in Angelo—

> *Immediate sentence then, and sequent death,*
> *Is all the grace I beg.*

In such states penalties may be pronounced by authority; they are invoked by the subject. The submissive is not passive only; it is on fire with love; it hastens to experience the great balance of sin and punishment—the words separate too much what becomes a unity. But in the State punishment is bound to seem, at least partly, self-preservation. The community penalizes offenders in order that it may itself live. It is not so in happier states; there, it may be said, punishment is love-preservation, and only self-inflicted. It was in relation to sin and pain that the Lady Julian said: "All shall be well, and all shall be well, and all manner of thing shall be well." Certainly in small things this can be seen; it is in the greater that it is difficult. It is true that the same Lady said that all our life was penance, and perhaps the burden of life might be eased if it were taken that way. "A kind soul hath no hell but sin."

All this belongs to the place of division. But it points to the place of union. Forgiveness is the way to the state of union and first appreciation of the state of union. It is so that it is seen (to return to Shakespeare) in those concluding scenes of the plays which, more than many religious books, make the great human reconcilement credible. In that poetry it remains, as do so many of the experienced mysteries, a wholly human thing. It has been said of Shakespeare that he wrote the whole supernatural life in terms of the natural, and it is true that he is the great protagonist of natural life without apparent need—humanly speaking—of the supernatural. It was a divine gift to us; he remains for ever a rebuke to the arrogant supernaturalists; they try to annex him, but it will not serve. He may or he may not have been religious in his personal life; he is not, when all is said, even when what has here been said about *Cymbeline* is said, religious in his poetry. But if anything of this nature could be deduced from his poetry the one thing that could be deduced would be that man's human nature was made on the same principles as his supernatural. He is, in that sense, as necessary to check the excesses of the disciples of Dante as Dante is to check the excesses of his disciples. Either without the other is incomplete; and it is not perhaps altogether by chance that Imogen and Beatrice are both the instruments and orators of pardon.

Endnotes

1. Canon O.C. Quick, *Christianity and Justice.*

THE DOCTRINE of LARGESSE

Review of *Forgiveness and Reconciliation: A Study in New Testament Theology* by Vincent Taylor; *Time and Tide*, December 6, 1941.

t may be that when the grooms and grocers, the gentlemen and jockeys and (as it were) chauffeurs of Constantinople argued at street-corners about the nomenclature of the Double-Natured One, the effect on the church was less than good. But we have some reason to think that the opposite state of affairs is no better. Emotionally, if not intellectually, we are still under the impression that the deeper theology goes, the simpler it ought to be. Yet the enjoyments of friendship are more subtle after years; and if our wives or husbands forgive us our debts (as they so often do), it does not follow that we have understood the whole of their complex love in the moment of the first renewed kiss.

"As below, so above." Even among Christians, the great experiences are often over-simplified, and the words *love* or *forgiveness* are thought to be sufficient. Obscurely resenting the theological disputes of the past, and not at all obscurely evading our moral duties in the future, we ask only that we shall act once and be done with it. The church was wiser; it provides for a monotony of pardon. It used to be blamed for compelling its members ritually to declare themselves "miserable sinners" day by day, but it knew very well that if they did not do it ritually they would not do it at all, and it very well knew what in fact they were. It oppressed them with a repentance they had half to feign in order that they should not feign a sufficiency which did not oppress them.

Dr. Taylor's book is an examination of the idea of pardon. It is theological; words which seem to us the dim echoes of evangelical tyrannies mean to him experiences of the soul; and of course he is right. The lack of those experiences in us does not falsify the high diagram. He examines the use of the word in the gospels, and concludes that it means less than it is usually taken to mean. It is "the bestowal of mercy and the cancellation of indebtedness." The restoration of normal relations, which is so often included in it, does not strictly belong to it at all. Before that pure restoration can take place, there must be not only a remission of debt but a communication of validity. Speaking in terms of human relations, it is this which causes the pardoner to recognize an equality in the pardoned; it is curious how apt this stage is to be overlooked, and a faint sense of superiority retained. I am not, of course, comparing the theological and human meanings; I am only illustrating. This is the prelude to a reconciliation—with God? doubtless, but say also with life, with living itself.

Dr. Taylor insists that modern theology is weak here, because, though it makes reconciliation central, it lays too much stress on what the death of Christ shows rather than on what it does. Like all acts, that act (since it was certainly he who permitted himself to die) exhibited a nature, but (more than all other acts) it produced, by itself, a result. It is therefore that acts done in union with that act have a unique validity. But that validity operates in the community, in the church, in the mystical body which rose, new-blooded, from the shed blood. "Only in the community can 'the individual' gain his individuality." "Sanctification" is that state in which "reconciliation and fellowship find their goal and consummation"; it is this which is, to raise to its full meaning a term otherwise applied, "the doctrine of largesse." "The language is sacrificial," says Dr. Taylor of other phrases concerned with "those who are sanctified," and the description is applicable to that phrase also. It was used originally of the Black Prince, who was said also to have a peculiar devotion to the Holy and Undivided Trinity. Whatever one's opinion of the Black Prince may be, the collocation of the two phrases has a great significance. The doctrine of the Trinity is a doctrine of largesse; the doctrine of the Atonement is a doctrine of largesse; the doctrine of the church is a doctrine of largesse; therefore the doctrine of the individual is a doctrine of largesse.

The operation which begins with the first kiss of pardon is not complete until all fibers of the being, physical and spiritual, are charged with that doctrine; and it is a doctrine of taking as well as of giving. It is easier often to forgive than to be forgiven; yet it is fatal to be willing to be forgiven by God and to be reluctant to be forgiven by men. To forgive and to be forgiven are the two points of holy magnificence and holy modesty; round these two centers the whole doctrine of largesse revolves. This is the pattern of our "actual situation" in the church, and "outside the church is no salvation." "I press on," wrote Saint Paul, "that I may apprehend that for which also I was apprehended by Christ Jesus." It is this full apprehension with which Dr. Taylor is concerned, and towards which he has provided a pattern of the Way.

THE CROSS

C.S. Lewis observed that there was in Williams a
strain of skepticism, even pessimism. No one's conversation was less gloomy in tone, but no one at
times said darker things. Something of that side of
him appears in this essay, originally published in
What the Cross Means to Me, a theological symposium (1943). Yet it ends, as a sermon might end, with
a Trinitarian ascription of praise.

ny personal statement on such a subject as the present is bound to be inaccurate. It is almost impossible to state what one in fact believes, because it is
almost impossible to hold a belief and to define it at
the same time, especially when that belief refers not
to objective fact but to subjective interpretation. A rhetorical
adjective will create a false stress; a misplaced adverb confuse
an emotion. All that can be hoped is that a not too incorrect
approximation may eventually appear. And anything that does
appear is, of course, to be read subject to the judgment of the
Christian church, by whom all individual statements must be
corrected.

Joseph Conrad, in his *Letters to Madame Paradowska,*
says: "Charity is divine and universal Love, the divine virtue,
the sole manifestation of the Almighty which may in some

manner justify the act of creation." The last phrase is not perhaps one which would be used by the normal Christian. But
the need for some such credible justification of the act of
creation is one of which even the normal Christian may, humanly speaking, be very conscious. Many sermons and pious
books are devoted to no other end. Much discussion of
"faith" means nothing else. Nor (still speaking in terms of human feeling) is such a justification unnecessary. The original
act of creation can be believed to be good and charitable; it is
credible that Almighty God should deign to create beings to
share his joy. It is credible that he should deign to increase
their joy by creating them with the power of free will so that
their joy should be voluntary. It is certain that if they have
the power of choosing joy in him they must have the power
of choosing the opposite of joy in him. But it is not credible
that a finite choice ought to result in an infinite distress; or
rather let it be said that, though credible, it is not tolerable
(to us) that the Creator should deliberately maintain and sus-
tain his created universe in a state of infinite distress as a result of the choice. No doubt it is possible to him.

This would be true, even if it were we ourselves who had
made that choice. I am far from saying that we did not. It may
be that we were "in" Adam very much more particularly than
is often supposed; it may be indeed that we, in that pre-fallen
state, *were* Adam, and that it was we who chose. *Fuimus ille
unus,* said Augustine, *quando fuimus in illo uno;* we were
the one when we were in the one. But popular doctrine in the
church has rather taken the view that we did not consciously
choose that original sin, but are at most its successors and inheritors. The vicarious guilt of it is in us; the derived concu-
piscence is in us. There remains for us the eternal dying
which is its result.

This is the law which his will imposed upon his creation. It
need not have been. Aquinas said that God wills his own

goodness necessarily, but other things not necessarily. Our distress then is no doubt our gratuitous choice, but it is also his. He could have willed us not to be after the Fall. He did not. Now the distress of the creation is so vehement and prolonged, so tortuous and torturing, that even naturally it is revolting to our sense of justice, much more supernaturally. We are instructed that he contemplates, from his infinite felicity, the agonies of his creation, and deliberately maintains them in it. I do not refer merely to the agonies of the present time; they are more spectacular and more destructive, but not more lasting, nor perhaps very much worse, than the agonies of a more peaceful time. But man has not often known a more peaceful time. And if he had, in the times that he has known, the very burden of daily existence too often seems a curse. The whole creation groaneth and travaileth together.

This then is the creation that "needs" (let the word be permitted) justifying. The cross justifies it to this extent at least—that just as he submitted us to his inexorable will, so he submitted himself to our wills (and therefore to his). He made us; he maintained us in our pain. At least, however, on the Christian showing, he consented to be himself subject to it. If, obscurely, he would not cease to preserve us in the full horror of existence, at least he shared it. He became as helpless as we under the will which is he. This is the first approach to a sense of justice in the whole situation. Whatever he chose, he chose fully, for himself as for us. This is, I think, unique in the theistic religions of the world. I do not remember any other in which the Creator so accepted his own terms—at least in the limited sense of existence upon this earth. It is true that his life was short, his pains (humanly speaking) comparatively brief. But at least, alone among the gods, he deigned to endure the justice he decreed.

There is another point of the same kind. It is often said that he was put to death by evil men. Caiaphas and Pilate and

Herod are denounced. It is, of course, in some sense true that it was evil which persecuted him. But I have myself felt that the destructiveness was more common to our experience if we hold, as we very well may, that Caiaphas and Pilate were each of them doing his best in the duty presented to them. The high priest was condemning a blasphemer. The Roman governor was attempting to maintain the peace. At the present time, for example, it is clear that one man must suffer for the people—and many more than one man, whether they consent or not. It is, no doubt, inevitable; it may be right. But we can hardly blame those earlier supporters of the same law. Humanly speaking, they were doing the best they could. They chose the least imperfect good that they could see. And their choice crucified the Good.

It is this agonizing fact which is too often present in our own experience. Certainly our sins and faults destroy the good. But our efforts after the good also destroy it. The very pursuit of goodness becomes a hunt; that which was to be our lord becomes a victim. It is necessary to behave well here? We do. What is the result? The destruction of some equal good. There is no more significant or more terrible tale in the New Testament than that which surrounded the young Incarnacy with the dying Innocents: the chastisement of his peace was upon them. At the end he paid back the debt—to God if not to them; he too perished innocently. With him also (morally) there was nothing else to be done.

He had put himself then to his own law, in every sense. Man (perhaps ignorantly, but none the less truly for that) executed justice upon him. This was the world he maintained in creation? *This* was the world he maintained in creation. This was the best law, the clearest justice, man could find, and he did well to accept it. If they had known it was he, they could have done no less and no better. They crucified him; let it be said, they did well. But then let it be said also, that the Sub-

limity itself had done well: adorable he might be by awful definition of his nature, but at least he had shown himself honor-
able in his choice. He accepted Job's challenge of long ago,
talked with his enemy in the gate, and outside the gate suffered (as the men he made so often do) from both his friends
and his enemies. Which of us has not known and has not
been a Judas? He had no where to lay his head? And we? "Behold my mother and my brethren."

This then has seemed to me now for long perhaps the most
flagrant significance of the cross; it does enable us to use the
word "justice" without shame—which otherwise we could not.
God therefore becomes tolerable as well as credible. Our justice condemned the innocent, but the innocent it condemned
was one who was fundamentally responsible for the existence
of all injustice—its existence in the mere, but necessary, sense
of time, which his will created and prolonged.

This is the more objective side; there is the more subjective. Man chooses, in most of his experiences, between the
rack and the cross, between a prolonged lesser and a shorter
but greater pain. I do not wish to seem here to become rhetorical; I do not underrate the great and pure beauties which
are presented and revealed to us, the virtue and value of fidelity, the appearance of a new kind of goodness where sometimes the old seems to have been exhausted. Yet it is also
true that a kind of death attends us all everywhere. Our best
knowledge is dimmed with boredom or darkened by destruction. "A mist goes up from the ground" or an earthquake
shakes it. A languor and a reluctance take us as we endure
the undestroyed good, or else the demand for its sacrifice pre-
occupies us. This occurs so often that we feel it to be in the
nature of life; this is what life is.

Yes then, certainly, this is what Life is. The cross is the exhibition of Life being precisely that; more—as knowing itself
to be precisely that, as experiencing itself as being precisely

that. We are relieved—may one say?—from the burden of being naturally optimistic. "The whole creation groaneth and travaileth together." If we are to rejoice always then it must be a joy consonant with that; we need not—infinite relief!—force ourselves to deny the mere burden of breathing. Life (experience suggests) is a good thing, and somehow unendurable; at least the Christian faith has denied neither side of the paradox. Life found itself unendurable. Romantically multiplying each side as our feelings may propose, we cannot go beyond that realism. Life itself consents to shrink from its own terrors; it concedes to us its utterance of our own prayer: "O not *this!* If it be possible, not *this!*" I am not for a moment equating our sorrows with that; the point is that the sorrow is centrally there. Life itself is acquainted with grief.

And not grief alone. Crucifixion was an obscene thing. It was revolting not merely because of the torture and the degradation, but also because of the disgust; or rather it is revolting to us—I do not know that it was revolting to those who saw it. They were as accustomed to it as our fathers were to burning and castration or we to many years' imprisonment or to the gallows. It was, however, definitely more spectacularly obscene than the gallows; we can hardly, in the nature of things, realize it so, and even our best efforts tend to make it a little respectable. But then again life, as we know it, is obscene; or, to be accurate, it has in it a strong element of obscenity. Again and again we become aware of a sense of outrage in our physical natures. Sometimes this is aroused by the events of which we read in the papers, but as often by the events which happen to us. The family, for example, is a sacred and noble thing, but the things that happen in the family are the result of blood antagonistic to itself. "Love," it is said, "is very near to hate." Without discussing the general truth of that, it may be allowed that where it is so, the hate is often of a particularly virulent and vehement kind.

I take these two qualities—the sorrow and the obscenity—as examples of that dreadful contradiction in our experience of life which is flatly exhibited in the living of life by Life. I am not unaware that it will be said that that which dies on the cross was something a great deal more than Life in any sense in which we understand the word. But I am not now talking of Christian dogma, but of a particular sense of the cross. "The feeling intellect" of the faith is a state of a much more advanced nature than anything I can claim to have known.

I say then that the idea of the cross does, on the one hand, make the idea of justice in God credible; and on the other certifies to us that we are not fools in being conscious of the twisting of all goodness to ignominy. We may (if it may be put so) approach God with that at least cleared up. We are not being unjust to his creation in the distaste we feel for it, nor even in the regret we feel that he allows it to continue. There would be other things to be said were we now discussing the Incarnation as such, but these are the things to be said peculiarly about the cross. This is what Almighty God, as well as we, found human life to be. We willed it so, perhaps, but then certainly he willed that we should will.

There is, however, more to it than that. There is Easter. It is not possible to separate the idea of Easter from the cross. Easter is its consequence. But it is a consequence of which many of us have very little apprehension. There are those who find it easy to look forward to immortality and those who do not. I admit that, for myself, I do not. It is true that the gradual stupefaction of the faculties which normally overcomes a man as he grows older seems to make—if not the idea of immortality more attractive—at least the idea of annihilation less so. Possibly curiosity is the last of one's faculties to be stupefied; possibly the natural egotism which has had a free run in one's life accentuates marvelously the idea of self-preservation as one approaches the apparent end of self-preservation. Possibly one is merely more fussy. Whatever is true, the idea of annihilation is more repellent. But I cannot say I find the idea of immortality, even of a joyous immortality, much more attractive. I admit, of course, that this is a failure of intelligence; if joy is joy, an infinite joy cannot be undesirable. The mere fact that our experience on this earth makes it difficult for us to apprehend a good without a catch in it somewhere, is, by definition, irrelevant. It may, however, make the folly more excusable.

Easter, however, is not only a consequence of the cross; it is also almost an accident of it. It followed the cross, but also it began in the cross. I say "in" rather than "on," for by the time it began he had become, as it were, the very profoundest cross to himself. That certainly he had always been prophetically, but now the exploration of his prophecies was complete. The cross was he and he the cross. His will had maintained, or rather his will in his Father's will had maintained, a state of affairs among men of which physical crucifixion was at once a part and a perfect symbol. This state of things he inexorably proposed to himself to endure; say, rather, that from the beginning he had been himself at bottom both the endurance and the thing endured. This had been true everywhere in all men; it was now true of himself apart from all men; it was local and particular. The physical body which was his own means of union with matter, and was in consequence the very cause, center, and origin of all human creation, was exposed to the complete contradiction of itself.

It would be perhaps too ingenious a fancy, which in these things above all is to be avoided, to say that actual crucifixion is a more exact symbol of his suffering than any other means of death. It is, however, with peculiar explicitness in the physical category what his other agony was in the spiritual (so, for a moment, to differentiate them). He was stretched, he was bled, he was nailed, he was thrust into, but not a bone of him was broken. The dead wood drenched with the blood, and the dead body shedding blood, have an awful likeness; the frame is doubly saved. It was the cross which sustained him, but he also sustained the cross. He had, through the years, exactly preserved the growth of the thorn and of the wood, and had indued with energy the making of the nails and the sharpening of the spear; say, through the centuries he had maintained vegetable and mineral in the earth for this. His providence overwatched it to no other end, as it over-watches so many instruments and intentions of cruelty then and now. The cross therefore is the express image of his will; it depends in its visible shape and strength wholly on him.

In the moment, as it were, of the final so-near-to-identity of himself and his wooden image, he spoke. He said: "It is fin-ished." It is at that moment that Easter began. It is not yet Easter; the Deposition has not yet taken place. He speaks, while yet he can, while he is not yet as speechless as the wood, and he announces the culmination of that experience. Life has known absolutely all its own contradiction. He sur-vives; he perfectly survives. His—I dare not call it victory—is not afterwards, but then. His actual death becomes almost a part of his resurrection, almost what Patmore called the death of the divine Mother, a "ceremony." Not so, for the ceremony was itself a work and a discovery, but then proper ceremonies are so; they achieve, as this does. The joy of his self-renewed knowledge perfectly exists, and his resurrection is (in his Father and Origin) at his own decision and by his own will. It is the will of his unalterable joy which, having ab-sorbed, exists.

This moment of consummation is therefore related to man's inevitable demand that all things should be justified in the moment that they happen. We must perhaps, joyously or reluctantly, consent to leave the knowledge of that justifica-tion till afterwards, but we must be willing to believe that it is

now. Or better, that the result is neither here nor there, neither now nor then, and yet both here and there, both now
and then. There has indeed been much admiration, much
gratitude, much love, that God should be made like us, but
then there is at least equal satisfaction that it is an unlike us
who is so made. It is an alien Power which is caught and suspended in our very midst. "Blessed be God," said John
Donne, "that He is God only and divinely like Himself." It is
that other kind of existence which here penetrates our hearts,
and is at all points credibly justified by our justice. The supreme error of earthly justice was the supreme assertion of
the possibility of justice. In his mortal life he never pretended, in making all his impossible and yet natural demands,
that he judged as we do. The parable of the laborers, the re-
ply to James and John, are alien from our equality; and so is
the incredible comment on Judas—"it were good for that man
if he had not been born." And who caused him to be born?
Who maintained his life up to and in that awful less than
good? It is in the gospels that the really terrifying attacks on
the gospel lie.

He was not like us, and yet he became us. What happened
there the church itself has never seen, except that in the last
reaches of that living death to which we are exposed he substituted himself for us. He submitted in our stead to the full
results of the Law which is he. We may believe he was generous if we know that he was just. By that central substitution,
which was the thing added by the cross to the Incarnation, he
became everywhere the center of, and everywhere he ener-
gized and reaffirmed, all our substitutions and exchanges. He
took what remained, after the Fall, of the torn web of humanity in all times and places, and not so much by a miracle of
healing as by a growth within it made it whole. Supernaturally he renewed our proper nature. By so doing, it is true, he
redoubled, at least within the church, our guilt and our dis-

tress. When he had made hope a virtue he had prevented it from being a natural habit. In all failures of love there is left to us only a trust in his work; that is what we call "faith," a kind of quality of action. It is, however, a trust in what is already done. Not only his act, but all our acts, are finished so. "Thy will be done on earth as it is in heaven" means precisely that at any moment the holy desire is already accomplished— not perhaps in the sense that we desire it, but in the sense that he wills it. It is finished; we too do but play out the necessary ceremony.

As in bombings from the air, cancer, or starvation, for instance? Yes, I suppose so; if at all, then certainly in those examples. The church (of which he seems to have had a low opinion) is his choice, but nature was his original choice, and he has a supreme fidelity. It is, in fact, that fidelity which causes him to maintain his creation and to die for his creation and to renew his creation. It may seem that little has been here said about our salvation through his sacrifice. That would not be quite true, for all that has been said concerns our salvation. Our salvation is precisely our reconciliation, to nature and to the church—not that they are so separate; our reconciliation both to him and to our present state, both at once and both in one. We are, by that august sacrifice, compelled to concede to him the propriety of our creation. I do not know that anything greater could be demanded or done.

"It is he that hath made us, and not we ourselves." We know that very well. But the General Thanksgiving ("general thanksgiving"—incredible words!) goes farther. "We bless Thee for our creation, preservation . . . for the means of grace and the hope of glory." It seems that nothing less will do. We are then required to do it because he does; it is at once a duty and a relief. Let him do it for us, for at least the Life in him is not separate from our life: we are allowed to repose in his blessing of himself, and to confirm ours by virtue of his blessing. The duty and the relief do not remain themselves; they are changed as nature is changed, as the elements in the eucharist are changed. In the eucharist he withdraws all into his resurrection, because the resurrection is in the sacrifice. This is not the place, however, to discuss the eucharist. It is sufficient to say that there, as everywhere, to be able to bless is to be in a state of salvation, in a state of goodwill towards him and all his creation, in a state of love. Only beatitude can properly bless, as only Love can love. In so far as we desire to bless, we are at least believers in a state of salvation now.

Our own guilt, natural or supernatural, is only manifested so. We can hardly be in a state of guilt towards something which is not in bearable relations with us. The crucifixion, restoring those relations, restores very much more. It permits repentance because it enables us to mean something by sin. Without that act, the infliction on us of something terribly like injustice would have made nonsense of any injustice on our side. He restores himself to us as God with all the qualities of God merely by being content not to be nothing but God. God can pardon, but pardon is only half pardon unless it is desired; the supreme life of it is precisely in the mutual act. There is no lovingness, mortal or divine, which does not, for its mutual quality, depend on that sacrifice of himself. "Others he saved; himself he cannot save." If he had saved himself, it seems, he could not have saved others; he did it by his power affirming, in the crucifixion, its own lack of power. He maintains us, by his will, in the state of sin in which we are; by his act he makes free to us the knowledge of that state, and of that issuing in him.

"O fools and slow of heart, *ought* not Christ to have suffered these things, and entered into his glory?" Yes; he ought. He said so: "The Son of Man *must....*" But then also he did. If the glory on which he insists, at such a cost, seems intolerable to us, if the exposition of release from our unhappy state seems as unbearable as the state itself, so that we cannot bear the only alternative to what we already cannot bear, at least that, after all, is the situation; it is he. We may be bold to say that he knows himself as well as we know him; after the cross we can believe that he knows himself not only as he does, but as we do. In the finishing of that knowledge a little cloud of fresh good arises, the first sense of that cloud into which he was received when he ascended. Whole, he died; whole, he rose; whole, he went up. Not the least gift of the gospel is that our experiences of good need not be separated from our experiences of evil, need not and must not be. In time they generally are, and even when they are not they are apt to seem unrelated. The authority which the good in our experience seems to have over us, unlike the evil, however much less than the evil it seems to be, is united with that other authority of the God who endured his own. It is the Christian religion that makes the Christian religion possible. Existence itself is Christian; Christianity itself is Christian. The two are one because he is, in every sense, life, and life is he. It is to that, in the Triune Unity, that there is ascribed, beyond all hope, to that only Omnipotence, as is most justly due, all might, majesty, dominion, and power.

THE WAY of EXCHANGE

As with "The Redeemed City," the occasion for this essay, published in 1941 as a pamphlet in a series called "New Foundations," was the war. Here Williams's concern, as always, is not so much with moral questions, important though they are, as with metaphysics—with the real nature of things, human and divine, as existing on each other's behalf.

I t has been of old a general complaint against war that it involves many harmless and unwilling persons belonging to different communities in the conflict between those communities. The general discussion whether we are at war with the German people or not is an example of this. Efforts have been made, and abandoned, to show that the German people are not at one with their leader. What is certain is that at present the vast majority of Europeans greatly dislike the conditions in which the vast majority of Europeans live. Nevertheless they assent, passively or actively, to the action of their governments; they are, so far, compelled to be at one with their governments. [...]

They and we are, in fact, committed by our governments. Those governments, in the nature of modern society, cannot be checked or much controlled, except at serious risk, by their nationals. We may well believe that the present situation

204

of Europe tends to show that our own government cannot have deceived us. But then we are still affected by the German government. We are at war because of Hitler, or because of the general tension between all governments; either way, we are not at war directly because of our own wish, but because of others. We depend upon others. The old cry against governments involving their peoples in war may be inapplicable in this war or not. It was sincere, but (as we now see) useless. We are always in the condition that we are because of others.

This is all so elementary as to sound stupid. Yet to accept this profoundly is difficult. To be in a distressing and painful condition because of others is a thing we all naturally resent. It is often the cause of hatred towards those others, whether in public or private things. Yet until we are willing to accept the mere fact without resentment we can hardly be said to admit that other people exist.

We may reject, we may rebuke, we may contend against their action. But the very first condition of admitting that their existence is as real as our own is to allow that they have, as individuals, as much right to act in the way that they decide as we have. They may be wicked and we good or vice versa; that is a question of moral judgment, and therefore another question. The main fact is that we are compelled to admit their decision, and to admit that our lives, and often our deaths, depend on that.

Such a decision, important as it is in war, is, in fact, no less important in peace. We have, first, to learn that others exist by ceasing to resent their existence. Until we have ceased to resent that existence, merely instinctively, we can hardly be said to admit it. But having admitted it, we have then to decide what we are to do about it; what our attitude is to be towards those other existences, what our relation with them. The great philosophies have given various answers; the great religions, on the whole, the same answer. Out of these the good taste of the West (one can hardly call it more) had, until recently, made a general amalgam which it called, roughly, "tolerance."

Tolerance meant, at worst, sullenly putting up with what one could not alter; at best, willingly accepting what one could not alter. It was a little limited by the fact that "to tolerate" was always considered as an active and hardly ever as a passive verb. One always tolerated and rarely was tolerated. The idea that others had, so to speak, to "put up with" oneself was rarely practiced, deeply and consistently. But, such as it is, toleration was, and remains, a noble virtue—yet a virtue which serves best as a guide to something greater than itself.

The great religions had, on the whole, recommended something more active. Much though they differed in their definitions of God, they did, generally, agree on their definitions of our duty towards our neighbor, even if they did not always agree on the exact definition of our neighbor. The Christian idea was expressed in the phrase "bear ye one another's burdens." It encouraged, indeed it demanded, a continual attention to the needs of one's neighbor, to his distresses and his delights. And it defined "neighbor" as meaning anyone with whom one was, by holy Luck, brought into contact. It required, then, an active "sympathy," and it spoke of something still higher, of an active and non-selfish love. It went even farther. It declared a union of existences. It proclaimed that our own lives depended on the lives of our neighbors. Saint Anthony of Egypt laid down the doctrine in so many words: "Your life and your death are with your neighbor."

August as that doctrine may have been, it is clear that it very soon became modified. It is regarded as Christian to live "for" others; it is not so often regarded as Christian doctrine that we live "from" others—except certainly in rare experi-

ences. There has been, everywhere, a doctrine of unselfishness, but that the self everywhere lives only within others has
been less familiar. The "bear one another's burdens" became,
on the whole, an exterior thing. We sympathized; we assisted.
We loved—from ourselves. But there had been more than that
in the original thought.

Certainly the great Christian doctrine applied first to the
"household of faith." Our Lord promised to the members of
his church a particular and intense union with each other
through himself. He defined that union as being of the same
nature as that which he had with his Father. The later definitions of the inspired church went farther; they declared not
merely that the Father and the Son existed co-equally, but
that they existed co-inherently—that is, that the Son existed *in*
the Father and that the Father existed *in* the Son. The exact
meaning of the preposition there may be obscure. But no
other word could satisfy the intellect of the church. The same
preposition was used to define our Lord's relations with his
church: "we in him and he in us." It was in that sense that
the church itself in-lived its children: "we are members one of
another."

It is not, however, entirely necessary to call the Christian
church in evidence that such is the nature of man. It was as
clear to the pagans that in society men depended on each
other exteriorly as it is to us. The whole natural and social
world depended, then as now, on some process of exchange.
Human life, in the Roman Empire, had been specialized; not
perhaps so much as ours, but it had been specialized. It depended on an exchange of labors. The medium of that exchange, with us, is money. Money has been called, by the
economists, "the means of exchange." Our social system exists by an unformed agreement that one person shall do one
job while another does another. Money is the means by which
those jobs are brought into relation. It is, usually, the me-

dium in which particular contracts are formed. And contract, or agreement, is the social fact of "living by each other."

This is the widest sense of social exchange. Within smaller groups—families or friends—the same thing is always taking place, sometimes irritably, sometimes happily. The more intense the element of love between two or more persons, the more clear, generally, that exchange of activities is. There certainly, in such states of natural love, doing it "for" someone else produces precisely that sense of increased well-being, of increased life, which the great doctrine asserts. The difference, of course, is that, in such cases of love, there have arisen naturally the conditions of goodwill towards the "neighbor"; where, however, those conditions do not naturally exist, love depends upon the will, and the difficulty of believing that we ourselves live by such acts is correspondingly greater, since the will does not, by itself, create emotion.

There is one great natural fact—a fact at the very root of all human facts—which involves a relation very much of the nature of exchange, or of something more than exchange. It is the fact of childbirth. Before any child can be born, the masculine seed has to be received by the feminine vessel. The man is quite helpless to produce a child unless he surrenders the means to someone else; the woman is as helpless unless she receives the means from someone else. It is a mutual act—but not only in the sense that two people agree to do something together. They do do something together, but they do it by an act (as regards the child) of substitution. It is not two people carrying a burden at the same time; the mother carries, literally, the burden. By the substitution of the woman for the man the seed fructifies. New life (literally) exists. It exists by the common operation of the woman and the man, and that operation involves something of the nature of substitution.

That substitution produces the new life. That new life exists literally within its mother; it inheres in its mother. The value of the sexual act itself is a kind of co-inherence; the two participators intend (violence apart) a renewal of mutual vigor from the most extreme intimacy of physical relationships. With conception comes the physical inherence of the child. And this is renewed through all the generations; each generation has inhered in that before it; in that sense without any doubt at all, we carry, if not another's burdens, at least the burden of others.

Such is the natural fact. At the root of the physical nature of man (so long as free choice exists) lie exchange of liking, substitution, inherence. The nature of man which is so expressed in the physical world is expressed after the same manner, only more fully, in the mental and spiritual.

The formal threefold division is a nuisance, but it may momentarily stand. What unites the three worlds is precisely this business of "living from others." In the mental world, for example, we derive nourishment, energy, and it is not perhaps going too far to say "life," from great art. Appreciation of great poetry, for example, gives us this sense that though we read and remember the lines, yet the lines are greater than we are and contain us—"felt in the blood and felt along the heart." It is not, however, in art, however great, that the secret lies; that cannot be more than a part of it. If this principle of exchange, substitution, and co-inherence (inhering in each other) is at all true, then it is true of the whole nature of man. If it is true, then we depend on it altogether—not as a lessening of individuality or moral duty but as the very fundamental principle of all individuality and of all moral duty.

In the records of the Thebaid, of the strange ascetic monks of the Egyptian desert, followers of Saint Anthony, the thing was put plainly enough.

A certain old man used to say, 'It is right for a man to take up the burden for those who are akin (or near) to him, whatsoever it may be, and, so to speak, to put his own soul in the place of that of his neighbour, and to become, if it were possible, a double man; and he must suffer, and weep, and mourn with him, and finally the matter must be accounted by him as if he himself had put on the actual body of his neighbour, and as if he had acquired his countenance and soul, and he must suffer for him as he would for himself.'

So great a business of exchange and substitution fills the phrase "bear ye one another's burdens" with a much fuller meaning than is generally ascribed to it. But that fuller meaning is no less practical than the usual meanings of being sympathetic and doing exterior acts "of kindness and of love." It is very proper that they should be done. But that is because we ought to be "members one of another"—*membra*, limbs, not members of the same society. Christians are not members of a club; they are "members" of the church, which is not a club. Men and women are not members of a club; they are "members" of mankind, which is not a club. From childbirth to those (in Dante's phrase) "adult in love," there is but one nature. That nature is not divided from grace; it is indeed (let it be said with submission to the theologians) the nature of grace. The difference, in that sense, is only a difference of power.

How then is this to be practiced? By "bearing one another's burdens" interiorly as well as exteriorly; by the turning of the general sympathy into something of immediate use; by a compact of substitution. It is the word "compact" that is to be stressed. I am not ignorant that in many cases such a substitution may take place instinctively, by the operation of an instinctive love; a wife for a husband, a lover for a lover, a friend for a friend. Still less am I ignorant of the great operations of this kind—in prayer and sacrifice—carried out by the religious orders. But we are not dealing here with the most intense states of natural love or with the most advanced sacrificial victims of religion, but with ourselves and with the ordinary man. It is ordinary life which might be, more than it is, shot with this principle; it requires only, I will not say faith, but the first faint motions of faith.

Compacts can be made for the taking over of the suffering of troubles, and worries, and distresses, as simply and as effectually as an assent is given to the carrying of a parcel. A man can cease to worry about X because his friend has agreed to be worried by X. No doubt this is only a part of casting all our burdens upon the Lord; the point is that it may well be a part of it. No doubt the first man may still have to deal directly with X; the point is that his friend may well relieve him of the extra burden. So also one may bind oneself more surely by promises made by another on one's behalf than by one's own promises; one may practice a virtue on behalf of another more easily than for oneself. The mere attention of the mind to such a life of substitution will itself provide instances and opportunities. What is needed is precisely that attention.

And, of course, common sense. There are as many dangers in that life as in any. We have to avoid portentousness; we have not to promise anything we obviously cannot do. But perhaps there is very little that could not be done. It does not follow that the payment must be made in the same kind as the original need. This is probably peculiarly true of physical needs. It is in small things that the practice could be begun— sleeplessness or anxiety or slight pains. It is between friends and lovers that the practice could be best begun; always remembering that in the end he whom holy Luck throws in our way is our neighbor—as much as (but perhaps not more than) he whom we go out of our way to seek. To begin the way in

small things conveniently is better than to dream of the remote splendors of the vicarious life; not that they are likely in
any case to seem very splendid when they come. To begin by
practicing faith where it is easiest is better than to try and
practice it where it is hardest. There is always somewhere
where it can be done.

The doctrine of the Christian church has declared that the
mystery of the Christian religion is a doctrine of co-inherence
and substitution. The divine Word co-inheres in God the Father (as the Father in him and the Spirit in both), but also he
has substituted his manhood for ours in the secrets of the Incarnation and Atonement. The principle of the Passion is that
he gave his life "for"—that is, instead of and on behalf of—
ours. In that sense he lives in us and we in him, he and we
co-inhere. "I live; yet not I but Christ liveth in me" said Saint
Paul, and defined the web of universal power towards substitution. To love God and to love one's neighbor are but two
movements of the same principle, and so are nature and
grace; and the principle is the Word by whom all things were
made and who gave himself for the redemption of all things.
It was precisely the breach in that original nature which the
new nature entered to fulfill. But either way it is our nature
that is concerned. Our natural life begins by being borne in
another; our mothers have to carry us. This is not (so far as
we know) by our own will. The Christian church demands
that we shall carry out that principle everywhere by our will—
with our friends and with our neighbors, whether we like our
neighbors or not.

Such a labor has, almost immediately, two results. In the
first place, it encourages a state of mind which may perhaps
be called humility—but not so much as a virtue as a mere fact.
Humility, said the author of the *Cloud of Unknowing*, consists in seeing things as they are. If our lives are so carried by
others and so depend upon others, it becomes impossible to

think very highly of them. In the second place there arises within one a first faint sense of what might be called "loving from within." One no longer merely loves an object; one has a sense of loving precisely from the great web in which the object and we are both combined. There is, if only transitorily, a flicker of living within the beloved. Such sensations are, or are not; they are, in themselves, of no importance. But they do for a moment encourage us, and they may assist us to consider still more intensely the great co-inherence of all life.

It is said (among other examples of substitution in the church) that the blessed Saint Seraphim of Sarov laid on a certain nun "the ascetic discipline of death, that she should die instead of her sick brother Michael, whose work was not yet done." The deaths of those of the English who are being killed every day are, in their manner, "instead of" us. Between the two the ladder lies by which our capacities run up and down, like angels; and the joy of the Word which is the ladder because of the Creation and the Incarnation and the Atonement sustains all. From childbirth to the divine Trinity itself the single nature thrives; there is here no difference between that natural and that super-natural.

Our chief temptation is to limit its operation. We can believe it happily of ourselves as regards our lovers and our friends; we can accept the idea, at least, as regards strangers; we cannot so easily as regards those of our "neighbors" who are, individually or nationally, inimical to us. We feel it as an outrage that we should be intimately interrelated, physically and spiritually, to those who have offended our pride or our principles; our very physical bodies revolt against it. It is why one hears of frustrated lovers committing murder; it is why our Lord warned us that murder was in our hearts. We desire to be free from the necessity of contemplating or practicing the awful truth. But the doctrine will not let us escape so. It is not for us to make a division; that power our Lord explicitly reserved to himself. If we insist on it, we can, in his final judgment, *be* separated. That is hell. But only our selves can put us there, and we cannot put others there. Virtue, in this as in all things, is merely to understand the republican fact.

It is republican because it exists everywhere and at all times. No civil or international war can alter it. No neglect of social duty can change it; if we are guilty of such a neglect then it will be we ourselves in whom the co-inherent life will tend to perish, and therefore we who will draw nearer to that "perishing everlastingly" which will one day be hell. The great rite of this (as of much else) within the Christian church is the eucharist, where the co-inherence is fully in action: "he in us and we in him." The prayer after communion in the ritual of the Church of England expresses it:

Almighty and everliving God, we most heartily thank thee, for that thou dost vouchsafe to feed us, who have duly received these holy mysteries, with the spiritual food of the most precious Body and Blood of thy Son our Saviour Jesus Christ; and dost assure us thereby of thy favour and goodness towards us; and that *we are very members incorporate in the mystical body of thy Son, which is the blessed company of all faithful people;* and are also heirs through hope of thy everlasting kingdom, by the merits of the most precious death and passion of thy dear Son. And we most humbly beseech thee, O heavenly Father, so to assist us with thy grace, *that we may continue in that holy fellowship, and do all such good works as thou hast prepared for us to walk in;* through Jesus Christ our Lord, to whom, with thee and the Holy Ghost, be all honour and glory, world without end.

The "good works which thou hast prepared for us to walk in" are those that belong to "that holy fellowship"; they are therefore those peculiarly of exchange and of substitution.

They are prepared and they are there; we have only to walk in them. A little carrying of the burden, a little allowing our burden to be carried; a work as slow, as quiet, even as dull as by agreement to take up or give up a worry or a pain—a compact of substitution between friends—this is the beginning of the practice. The doctrine will grow in us of itself.

THE PRACTICE of SUBSTITUTED LOVE

This collection began with an essay setting out the theological context of Williams's thinking. It ends here with one that recapitulates many of the components of "the pattern of the glory" as he perceived it. This was originally the sixth chapter of *He Came Down from Heaven*.

mong the epigrams of the kingdom which Saint John arranged in his gospel immediately before the triumph of the kingdom, he attributed to Messias the saying: "Greater love hath no man than this that a man lay down his life for his friends." It is, on a second glance, a doubtful truth. Many men have exhibited their will of love in such a surrender, but many—perhaps more—have exercised among all kinds of hardship a steady tenderness of love besides which the other seems almost easy. But the phrase has to be understood in the context of other meanings. The "greater love" is distinguished by the "laying down the life": something similar had been decreed at Sinai: "thou shalt not see my face, for there shall no man see me and live." The definition does not, in the gospels, necessarily mean physical death, even if that is sometimes involved. When Mes-

sias said: "Whosoever will lose his life for my sake and the
gospel's, the same shall find it," he did not confine the promise to the martyrs nor deny to Saint John what he allowed to
Saint James. Martyrdom might or might not happen. Saint
Paul, in the passage already quoted [1 Corinthians 13:3], denied any value at all to martyrdom unless it were accompanied by *caritas:* "though I give my body to be burned and
have not charity, it profiteth me nothing." According to the
Apostle, self-sacrifice by itself was as remote from the way of
salvation as self-indulgence. As a technique, as a discipline, as
a method, it might be useful: no more. But so may—if not self-
indulgence at least things gratifying to the self. We are not to
deny to others the means of their love because those means
may seem to indulge us. "Neither Jew nor Greek, but a new
creature." Neither self-sacrifice, as such, nor self-gratification,
as such; both may be sacraments of love at any moment, but
neither is covenanted. The denial of the self affects both. "It
is no more I that live, but Christ that liveth in me" is the definition of the pure life which is substituted for both.

The taunt flung at that Christ, at the moment of his most
spectacular impotency, was: "he saved others; himself he cannot save." It was a definition as precise as any in the works of
the medieval schoolmen. It had been already accepted by the
action—the action which restrained action—of Messias, as it
had been accepted still earlier by his words when he chose
necessity. It was an exact definition of the kingdom of heaven
in operation, and of the great discovery of substitution which
was then made by earth. Earth, at best till then under the
control of law, had to find that no law was enough unless the
burden of the law, of the law kept or the law unkept, could be
known to be borne by heaven in the form of the Holy Thing
that came down from heaven. Earth had to find also that the
new law of the kingdom made that substitution a principle of
universal exchange.

The first canon of substitution had been declared in the myth of origin ages before, when the law of man's responsibility for man had been shaped. It had denounced there the first-born child of the Adam, though of the Adam no longer in the union of the knowledge of the good, but in the divided sorrow of conception and of work. The child was Cain, the incarnation of their union outside paradise, and in some sense of the self-desirous spirit which troubles the divine glory in all lovers. An opposition to goodness was in his nature and is in theirs, a desire to trouble goodness with some knowledge of some kind of evil. He not only killed his brother; he also made an effort to carry on the intellectual falsity which his parents had experienced when they fled from facts in their new shame. He became rhetorical—it is, so early, the first appearance of a false style of words: "Am I my brother's keeper?" It is a question asked by most people at some moment. "The voice of thy brother's blood crieth unto me from the ground." That answer became a law in the covenants: "At the hand of every man's brother will I require the life of man."

As the single tyranny of Cain developed into the social tyranny in Egypt and in Israel itself, so the law gathered round itself the clamor of the prophets for social justice: "seek judgment, relieve the oppressed, judge the fatherless, plead for the widow...what mean ye that ye beat my people to pieces, and grind the faces of the poor? saith the Lord God of hosts." Under the organized effort of Rome towards at least something of the Virgilian equity, this had been defined in the moral duty of all classes and individuals declared by the Precursor; it had become the gospel of the Precursor as of Virgil, except that the one gospel expected beyond itself what the other hardly could. Messias had shown that he would demand and assume its fulfillment by all who wished to follow his own gospel. It had to be left, then, to men to choose or not to choose. The direct concern of the new kingdom was with other things, with the love that had substituted itself for men, and with the love between men that was to form itself after the manner of that original love.

When Messias removed his visibility, he left behind him a group of united followers; he had created the church. If the Acts of the Apostles are any guide—say in chapters 2, 3, 4—the church began with direct statements of dogma and direct communication of rites. Necessarily, as it spread, it had to organize itself; it had to make decisions on fundamental questions. There was the question, as it grew, of what on certain points it did actually believe; it answered this by finding out in its councils what in fact it did—in its various localities—actually believe. The message of the councils to the localities after an inquiry tended to be not so much "we are telling you what is true" as "it has been decided that *this* is what the church actually believes." Certainly, by rapid development of a hypothesis of its nature, the two things became identical, but there was a difference in method and indeed in idea. Occasionally a council came to a decision which was not accepted, in which case the hypothesis sooner or later involved the view that it was not a proper council. For the hypothesis was that there was operative within the church the sacred and eternal reconciliation of all things, which the church did not and could not deserve. The church (it was early decided) was not an organization of sinless men but of sinful, not a union of adepts but of less than neophytes, not of *illuminati* but of those that sat in darkness. Nevertheless, it carried within it an energy not its own, and it knew what it believed about that energy. It was the power of the Reconciler, and the nature of the Reconciler was of eternity as of time, of heaven as of earth, of absolute God as of essential Man. "Let those who say *There was when he was not* be anathema."

There was then, so to put it, a new way, the way of return to blissful knowledge of all things. But this was not sufficient; there had to be a new self to go on the new way. This was the difficulty of the church then as it is now, as it always is after any kind of conversion. There are always three degrees of consciousness, all infinitely divisible: (1) the old self on the old way; (2) the old self on the new way; (3) the new self on the new way. The second group is the largest, at all times and in all places. It is the frequent result of romantic love. It forms, at any one moment, the greatest part of the visibility of the church, and, at most moments, practically all of oneself that one can know, for the new self does not know itself. It consists of the existence of the self, unselfish perhaps, but not yet denied. This self often applies itself unselfishly. It transfers its activities from itself as a center to its belief as a center. It uses its angers on behalf of its religion or its morals, and its greed, and its fear, and its pride. It operates on behalf of its notion of God as it originally operated on behalf of itself. It aims honestly at better behavior, but it does not usually aim at change; and perhaps it was in relation to that passionate and false devotion that Messias asked: "Think ye when the Son of Man cometh he shall find faith upon the earth?"

Those who accuse the church accuse it—justly—of not being totally composed of new selves; those who defend it defend it—justly—as being a new way. No doubt the old self on the new way is a necessary period, in most cases, of change. But the apostles, to judge by the epistles, were not willing that the faithful should remain consistently faithful to themselves. They demanded, as Messias had demanded, that the old self should deny itself. It was to be removed and renovated, to be a branch of the vine, a point of the pattern. It was to become an article of love. And what then is love?

It is possible here to follow only one of the many definitions the New Testament holds; the definition of death. To love is to die and live again; to live from a new root. Part of the experience of romantic love has been precisely that; the experience of being made new, the "renovation" of nature, as Dante defined it in a particular experience of love. That experience is not sufficient to maintain itself, or at least does not choose to do so. But what is there experienced, and what has been otherwise experienced by many in religion, or outside religion, has to be followed by choice. "Many are called but few are chosen": we are called from the kingdom but we choose from ourselves. The choice is to affect not only our relation with God but our relation with men. There is to be something of the same kind of relation in it. "These things have I spoken unto you, that my joy might remain in you, and that your joy might be full." It is odd how rarely Messias is seen as full of joy—but there it is. He said so; no one else. He proceeded towards our joy: "This is my commandment, that ye love one another, as I have loved you."

The first epistle of Saint John carried the same idea, and the Revised Version has it more sharply than the Authorized. "Hereby know we love, because he laid down his life for us, and we ought also to lay down our lives for the brethren...if we love one another, God abideth in us, and his love is perfected in us." We are to love each other *as* he loved us, laying down our lives *as* he did, that this love may be perfected. We are to love each other, that is, by acts of substitution. We are to be substituted and to bear substitution. All life is to be vicarious—at least, all life in the kingdom of heaven is to be vicarious. The difference between life in the kingdom and life outside the kingdom is to be this. "Except your righteousness exceed the righteousness of the Scribes and Pharisees, ye shall in no wise enter into the kingdom of Heaven." But many of the Scribes and Pharisees were good and holy men? yes;

what then? it is this love-in-substitution, this vicarious life, which is no more in their law than in the gospel of the Precursor. "Go, tell John, the blind receive their sight...the least in the kingdom of heaven is greater than he."

It has been the habit of the church, since the earliest times, ostentatiously to use some such substitution, in one rite at least: in the baptism of infants. It is understood that this is largely due to the persecutions, but also to the nature of the sacrament itself; which was purposed for infants as well as adults, and yet demanded penitence and faith before its operation could be ensured. This responsibility was laid on the godparents: "at the hand of every man's brother will I require the life of man." But it is others than infants who can swear more sincerely and more humbly by others' mouths than ever by their own, though it must be with the agreement and desire of their own. It is one of the difficulties of the church that her presentation of experience does not always coincide with realized experience. The conversion she demands and the sustenance she communicates come sometimes from alien and even from hostile sources; it is one conversion and one sustenance with hers. The invisible church moves in another manner than the visible; indeed the invisible must include that earthly skepticism, opposition which the visible church so greatly needs and yet cannot formally include. The sponsors in baptism exhibit the idea of substitution, as that habit which existed in the early church of being baptized "for the dead" exhibited it. Part of the fact which such an exhibition ritually and sacramentally presents is the making a committal of oneself from another's heart and by another's intention. It is simpler sometimes and easier, and no less fatal and blessed, to do it so; to surrender and be offered to destiny by another rather than by oneself; it is already a little denial of the self.

But that is as holy Luck may decide. Whatever the means of beginning, the life itself is vicarious. The courtesies of that life are common enough—to lend a book, for example, is a small motion in it, an article of the web of glory. It is the full principle which is defined by the New Testament, and the making of contracts on that principle which exhibit, in the denial of self, the pattern of the web.

Saint Paul, in one of those letters which are at once mystical diaries, archiepiscopal charges, and friendly messages, threw out an instruction to the church at Galatia (Gal. 6:2). "Bear ye one another's burdens, and so fulfill the law of Christ." It is, like the patience of Job, one of our most popular texts. In exterior things it is recognized as valid—at least until we become bored; the fiftieth rather than the first visit to the sick is distasteful. Interiorly, it is less frequently supposed to be possible, and even exteriorly it has a wider range than is, perhaps, allowed. Saint Paul's injunction is to such acts as "fulfill the law of Christ," that is, to acts of substitution. To take over the grief or the fear or the anxiety of another is precisely that; and precisely that is less practiced than praised. "Mystical substitution" we have heard from the textbooks, or from other books that are less than the textbooks. It is supposed to be for "nuns, confessors, saints, not us": so much the worse for us. We are supposed to be content to "cast our burdens on the Lord." The Lord indicated that the best way to do so was to hand these over to someone else to cast, or even to cast them on him in someone else. There will still be work enough for the self, carrying the burdens of others, and becoming the point at which those burdens are taken over by the Divine Thing which is the kingdom: "as he is, even so are we in this world."

The technique needs practice and intelligence, as much intelligence as is needed for any other business contract. The commerce of love is best established by commercial contracts with man. If we are to make agreements with our adversaries quickly, we ought to be even quicker to make them with our friends. Any such agreement has three points: (1) to know the burden; (2) to give up the burden; (3) to take up the burden. It is perhaps in this sense also that Messias said: "Deny the self, take up the cross, follow me"; it being admitted and asserted that the crucifixion itself is his. He flung out those two seemingly contradictory assertions, he who was rich in contradictions: "take up the cross," "my yoke is easy, and my burden is light." It is not till the cross has been lifted that it can be a burden. It is in the exchange of burdens that they become light. But the carrying of a cross may be light because it is not to the crucifixion. It is "of faith" that that is done; that is, it is the only part of the work still to be done that we should be fitted into the state where all is done, into the kingdom and the knowledge of everything as good. But a pride and self-respect which will be content to repose upon Messias is often unapt to repose on "the brethren." Yet that too is part of the nature of all and of the action of the contract.

The one who gives has to remember that he has parted with his burden, that it is being carried by another, that his part is to believe that and be at peace; "brother, our will is quiet in the strength of love...herein love is fate." The one who takes has to set himself—mind and emotion and sensation—to the burden, to know it, imagine it, receive it—and sometimes not to be taken aback by the swiftness of the divine grace and the lightness of the burden. It is almost easier to believe that Messias was probably right about the mysteries of the Godhead than that he was merely accurate about the facts of everyday life. One expects the burden always to be heavy, and it is sometimes negligible; which is precisely what he said. Discovering that, one can understand more easily the happy abuse he flung at the disciples, say, at the two who went to Emmaus. "Then he said unto them, O fools and slow of heart to believe all that the prophets have spoken: ought not Christ to have suffered these things and have entered into his glory? And beginning at Moses and all the prophets he expounded unto them in all the scriptures the things concerning himself."

The giver's part may be harder than the taker's; that is why, here, it may be more blessed to give than to receive, though in the equity of the kingdom there is little difference. It has a greater tendency towards humility and the intellectual denial of the self. In all the high pagan philosophies, now as then, there are many great virtues, and their leaders and teachers often were and are holy and humble men of heart. I do not remember that any of them cried out: "See how meek and lowly I am!" No Christian has been encouraged to murmur of himself in that state which is called "the inner chamber" what Christ proclaimed of himself to the world. It is the everlasting difference between the gospel of Christ as one who is to be imitated and one who is to be believed, between one who is an example of living and one who is the life itself; between the philosophies that advise unselfishness as the best satisfaction in life and the religion that asserts exchange to be the only possible means of tolerable life at all. The denial of the self has become metaphysical. He came to turn the world upside-down, and no one's self-respect will stand for that. It is habitual to us therefore to prefer to be miserable rather than to give, and to believe that we can give, our miseries up.

There is, of course, a technique. If *A* is to carry *B*'s burden he must be willing to do it to the full, even though he may not be asked to do it to the full. It is easy to sentimentalize, but the Day of Judgment exhibits our responsibilities in each case: "at the hand of every man's brother will I require...." Messiah may, now, carry the burden if we ourselves deliberately neglect or forget the agreement, but the lucidity of the good knowing the evil as good is likely to exhibit the negligence or forgetfulness as much as the substitution of himself. It is therefore necessary (*a*) not to take burdens too recklessly; (*b*) to consider exactly how far any burden, accepted to the full, is likely to conflict with other duties. There is always a necessity for intelligence.

Our reluctance is inevitably encouraged by the difficulty of carrying out this substitution in the physical world; of developing between men the charismatic ministry. The body is probably the last place where such interchange is possible; it is why Messias deigned to heal the body "that ye may know that the Son of Man hath power *on earth* to forgive sins." No such exchange is possible where any grudge—of pride, greed or jealousy—exists, nor any hate; so far all sins must have been "forgiven" between men. In some states of romantic love it is felt that the power of healing exists, if only it could be brought into action, and on the basis of Romantic Theology it could so be brought into action. We habitually expect too little of ourselves. But it is not only in states of realization that the power exists. It is limited, peculiarly, by other duties. Most men are already so committed that they ought not, whatever their goodwill, to contemplate the carrying of the burden of paralysis or consumption or even lesser things. They are still bound to prefer one good to another. Certainly it is reasonable to believe that the kind of burden might be transmuted into another equivalent kind, and in a full state of the kingdom upon earth such a transmutation would be agreeable and natural. It remains at present an achievement of which our "faith" is not yet capable. That is no reason why we should not practice faith, a faith in the interchange of the kingdom operating in matter as out of matter, because whatever distinction there may be between the two is only a distinction between modes of love.

It is natural that, in certain happy states (*e.g.,* the Beatrician love), there should be a desire to make any contract of the kind mutual, and so it often may be. At the same time the tendency is sometimes for the pattern not to return but to proceed. The old proverb said that there was always one who kissed and one who took kisses; that too, accepted, is in this sense a part of the pattern. The discovery that one cannot well give back or be given back what one has given or been given in the same place is sometimes as painful as the discovery that one is being loved on principle and not from preference: a good deal of conviction of the equality of all points in the web of the kingdom and of the denial of the self is necessary to make it bearable. Man—fallen man—has, oddly, the strongest objection to being the cause of the practice of *caritas* by someone else. Yet the apostles in their epistles continually, and necessarily, exhort the faithful to the practice of such a submission: "let us not love in word, neither in tongue, but in deed and in truth." To be grateful for what one does not want is a step towards love, even if it is the rather difficult gratitude for the smirk of a well-meaning intercession by the official twice-born in the visible church. Gratitude is a necessity of all life; it is love looking at the past as faith is love intending the future, and hope is the motion of the shy consciousness of love in the present self; and gratitude, like love, is its own sufficiency:

> *a grateful mind*
> *By owing owes not but still pays, at once*
> *Indebted and discharged.*[1]

It is with the intention of substituted love that all "intercessory" prayer must be charged, and with care that there is no intention of emotional bullying. Even prayer for the conversion of others is apt to be more like prayer for their conversion to the interceder's own point of view than to the kingdom. The old self on the new way has always enjoyed himself most at prayer. He can pray fervently for other people's delivery from other people's sins; he can indicate to Messias where X is wrong; he can try and bring supernatural power to bear on X to stop him or divert him or encourage. It is precisely because he is playing with a real power that this is so dangerous. It is dangerous, for example, to pray that Nero may be delivered from killing Agrippina; it looks a fairly safe petition but....What do we know of Nero, of Agrippina, of Messias? But it can never be dangerous, without particularizing, without fluency, intensely to recollect Nero and Agrippina "in the Lord," nor can it be dangerous to present all pains and distresses to the kingdom with the utmost desire that Messias may be, and the recollection that at that moment he is, the complete reconciliation—through the point that prays, if conditions are so, but if not then through all and any of the points of the kingdom.

"All and any." We operate, mostly, in sequence, but sequence is not all. "I am Alpha and Omega, the first and the last, the beginning and the end." There is no space here to discuss theories of time or the nature of the intercession of the saints. The vicarious life of the kingdom is not necessarily confined to sequence even among the human members of the kingdom. The past and the future are subject to interchange, as the present with both, the dead with the living, the living with the dead. "The living creatures ran and returned, as the appearance of a flash of lightning." The laying down of the life is not confined, in the universal nature of the Sole-Begotten, to any points of space or time. It flashes and returns, in a joy, in a distress, and often without joy or distress. Along such threads the glory runs, and along what are, at present, even fainter threads than those.

The method of the new life which Messias (he said) came to give so abundantly begins with substitution and proceeds by substitution. No such substitution accents the individual less; on the contrary, it is, for most, the strongest life of the individual. Even in the kingdom of this world those are greatest who (rightly or wrongly) have had assessed to them the desires, wills, lives of others, when Caesar was Rome and Napoleon was France. It is the touch of impersonality in Caesar, the hint that he had in his own strange way denied the self and become only Caesar even to himself that makes him so fascinating. His star burns on the ancient world, as Virgil saw it at Actium, over the homes, the families, the *pietas* of man, before it is answered by the other star that proclaimed the kingdom of a greater substitution.

In the old days David, or whoever wrote the psalm, exclaimed that no man could redeem or give a ransom for his brother, and in the ultimate sense that is so still, but it was said before the revelation of the secret of evil known as good, and before the mystery of the Atonement of Messias had brought all things into the pattern of the Atonement. All goodness is from that source, changed and exchanged in its process. It was said of the friars that one went patched for another's rending, and in the kingdom men go glorious for others' labors, and all grown glorious from the labor of all. Messias, after he had spoken to the astonished soul of the five husbands that she had had, and none of them all he—no, not the present lover, however righteous, however holy, he— spoke yet more riddles to the returning apostles. He looked on the fields, he saw them white to harvest, he cried out of wages and fruit and eternal life, and at once of him that sowed and him that reaped and their common joy. And even as he said it, he flung his words into a wider circuit: "herein is that saying true, one soweth and another reapeth. I sent you to reap that whereon ye bestowed no labor: other men labored and ye are entered into their labors."

What! after self-sacrifice and crosses and giving up goods
and life, the mind perplexed, the heart broken, the body
wrecked—is there not a little success of our own, our own in
him, of course, but at least his in us? None; "I sent you to
reap that whereon ye bestowed no labor." The harvest is of
others, as the beginning was in others, and the process was
by others. This man's patience shall adorn that man, and that
man's celerity this; and magnificence and thrift exchanged;
and chastity and generosity; and tenderness and truth, and so
on through the kingdom. We shall be graced by one and by
all, only never by ourselves; the only thing that can be ours is
the fiery blush of the laughter of humility when the shame of
the Adam has become the shyness of the saints. The first and
final maxim in the present earth is *deny the self*, but—there or
here—when the need for denial has passed, it may be possible
to be astonished at the self as at everything else, when that
which is God is known as the circle whose center is everywhere and the circumference nowhere. "He saved others; himself he cannot save." "The glory which thou gavest me I have
given them; that they may be one, even as we are one: I in
them, and thou in me, that they may be made perfect in one."

Endnotes

1. Milton, *Paradise Lost*, IV 55.

OWLEY PUBLICATIONS is a ministry of the Society of St. John the Evangelist, a religious community for men in the Episcopal Church. Emerging from the Society's tradition of prayer, theological reflection, and diversity of mission, the press is centered in the rich heritage of the Anglican Communion.

Cowley Publications seeks to provide books, audio cassettes, and other resources for the ongoing theological exploration and spiritual development of the Episcopal Church and others in the body of Christ. To this end, it is dedicated to developing a new generation of theological writers, encouraging them to produce timely, creative, and stimulating publications of excellence, and making these publications available widely, reaching both clergy and lay persons.